Wrapped

in the

Light

31 Morning
& Evening
Devotions

D1214099

Wrapped in the Light
31 Morning & Evening Devotions
©2021 by Gina Lynn Murray and Ellen Sallas
All rights reserved.

Little Roni Publishers
Clanton, Alabama
www.littleronipublishers.com

ISBN: 978-1-7359337-8-8 | Also available in eBook
V.11172021
Cover Image: ©DepositPhotos/WelComia
Back cover Image © DepositPhotos/AlexKich
Interior Cutout Snowflake © DepositPhotos/paprika
Cover & Interior Design: Ellen Sallas

For editorial requests or to purchase multiple copies at wholesale, contact the Editor at SubmissionsLRP@gmail.com.

PUBLISHED IN THE UNITED STATES OF AMERICA

2022

This book belongs to

Jan

My precious cousin
and dearest friend ♡
I love you!
Jenny

Jesus said, "I am the Light of the world. Whoever follows Me will never walk in darkness, but will have the Light of Life." John 8:12

1

LEAN IN, CLOSE YOUR EYES, & REST

Then Jesus said, "Come to Me, all of you who are weary and carry heavy burdens, and I will give you rest. Take My yoke upon you. Let Me teach you, because I am humble and gentle at heart, and you will find rest for your souls. For My yoke is easy to bear, and the burden I give you is light."

Matthew 11:28-30 NLT

Jesus wants to help you. He knows we cannot rest if we're weighed down with life's troubles. We cannot enjoy life if we carry burdens to bed and awake with them still over our heads.

When you yoke yourself with Jesus, you are never alone. He carries us when we do not have the strength to carry on and stands ready to help us with life's struggles. Rest in Him. He is beside you every moment. He never rejects you or walks away. He is *continually* wanting to commune with you, constantly inviting you into His presence!

Pour out your heart to Him; allow Him to heal your wounds. Fix your eyes on Jesus and let Him teach you how to take a *real rest.*

Let Him restore your life and refresh your spirit. He wants to wrap His love around you like a warm blanket on a cold winter's night. You can talk to Him anytime and anywhere. Even if you don't have the words to say, just sit with Him and rest your mind.

Nothing in this world can give you peace like the Prince of Peace. The "peace" the world offers is false, fleeting, and based upon our circumstances. But the peace of Jesus has nothing to do with our circumstances and everything to do with Him.

Wrap yourself in His blanket of love. Cozy up and allow Him to pour out His rest and His peace on your mind and your heart. Allow it to soak through every fiber of your being. Take a deep breath and whisper His name. It is sweeter than the sweetest honey on your lips. Lean in, close your eyes, and rest.

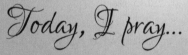

Today, I pray...

This stressful situation is on my mind:

_____.

I know You have this well in hand.
I know You will work Your will in this matter.
I know Your will is perfect & good.
Help me to understand what You are doing.
Teach me how to hear and obey Your will.
I love you and I need you,
Amen.

Fear Not for I Am with You

So do not fear, for I am with you; do not be dismayed, for I am your God. I will strengthen you and help you; I will uphold you with my righteous right hand.

Isaiah 41:10 NIV

When God tells us, do not be afraid, the first thing to notice is that **He understands that we're afraid.** We live in the flesh, we will become frightened, we will have anxiety, we will worry for ourselves and others. In the context of this verse, God is encouraging Israel to *not be afraid* for an obvious reason—because HE IS GOD.

Allow me to paraphrase. "Beloved, don't be afraid of anything out there in the world. I made you, I made the enemy, and I made the entire universe. I am capable and willing to keep you safe, and I promise that I will do so."

What blows me away is the sentiment just before verse 10: **"I have chosen you and have not rejected you."** That is HUGE! If you know Jesus, it is because you have been CHOSEN to know Him. It was HIS doing, not yours, that you two met up!

BUT-BUT-BUT- No buts. We will have trials and tribulations in this life, but with each one, you can **turn to God and ask Him to help you.**

3

"TRUST GOD." People outside the family of God scoff at this phrase. But we know that fear comes from the adversary, satan[1], and that **Jesus did not give us a spirit of fear.**

WHY can we trust God? Because He said so. **But what if I get hurt?** You might. You probably will, but He uses these pains to strengthen us, build our relationship with Him, and sometimes, to chastise or correct us on our path.

Ask God to reveal why you were entered into the current trial. God's ways are high above our own, but you can rely on Him to know what He's doing—He is doing it for your own good. And that is a fact you can depend on.

Tonight, I pray...

Father, help me, I'm scared. Please help me to see what You are doing. Give me the wisdom and knowledge of God to comprehend WHY. Please enable me to be patient, growing my faith every day.

Amen

2

JESUS SATISFIES YOUR SPIRITUAL THIRST

Jesus replied, "If you only knew the gift God has for you and who you are speaking to, you would ask Me, and I would give you living water. Anyone who drinks this water will soon become thirsty again. But those who drink the water I give will never be thirsty again. It becomes a fresh, bubbling spring within them, giving them eternal life."

John 4:10, 13-14 NLT

There are times when everything looks dry, dead, and barren, and you aren't sure if these things will ever live again. Your soul is so thirsty! You tried to satiate this longing with material things, friends, travel, or maybe even work. **But there is only One who can satisfy,** only One who gives Living Water. And, He not only satisfies you for today, but for eternity.

Jesus is the answer you seek. Jesus is the Messiah, the Son of God, the Savior of the world; when His Living Water bubbles up inside of you, you can't help but let it overflow. Watch and see! It changes your perspective so much that even in your darkest days, you can walk in joy. All you have to do is ask. **Jesus will never turn anyone away.**

Unlike a pond that sits and becomes stagnant, the Living Water flows continually, constantly refreshing everything it envelops.

The Living Water is a healing balm. **Allow it to completely submerge the fractures in your life.** Watch as it brings the pieces back together.

Come! Every day, sit with Jesus, ask for this Living Water, and drink deeply. You will find you have been quenched!

Today, I pray...

Father, this Living Water that I read of in Your word... I want that. *I need that!* Please, give me the Living Water of Jesus. I ask for it, and I drink of it, right now in Jesus' name. Your Living Water is a refreshing spring within me RIGHT NOW, and I thank You. As I begin my day, enable me to know & understand You more and more every waking minute! I love you! Amen.

Jesus Holds it Together

For in Him all things were created: things in heaven and on earth,
visible and invisible, whether thrones or powers or rulers or authorities;
all things have been created through Him and for Him. He is before
all things, and in Him all things hold together.
Colossians 1:16-17 NIV

What in the world does that mean, "in Him, all things hold together"? I wondered this the first time I read that verse and I did a little digging. Turns out, it means precisely what it sounds like; COHERE. The Greek word used here means *cohere, stick together, cling together.*

Think about that... **Because of Jesus, everything in the world COHERES.** Because of Jesus, our world doesn't literally fly apart. No matter the varying semantic nuances, the fact remains and it carries *tremendous depth* regarding the omnipotence of God.

In this verse, Paul wants us to know that the entire universe, everything visible and invisible, was created *for* Jesus, **to bring glory to His name.**

7

How could it be that the world was created *through* Jesus? Remember, in Genesis, *God spoke the world into existence.*[2] Who is the Word of God? Jesus Christ the Messiah![3] The Savior of the world. Omniscient, omnipotent, and omnipresent, right here in these two verses.

What it means for us is that we are in excellent Hands. Our King, our God, our Everything *is in control.* He is just. He is good. His will is done on earth as it is in heaven, and His will is perfect all the time. Rest easy, beloved!

Tonight, I pray...

Father, tonight I learned that it's because of You that everything holds together. Thank You for that! Also, I was reminded that the entire universe was created specifically for Your glory—that YOU might be glorified in the workings of Creation. Thank You for watching over me as I sleep and when I wake, show me how to glorify You in my daily walk. I love you! Amen

3

JESUS HAS BEEN THERE/DONE THAT

Therefore, since we have a great high priest who has ascended into heaven Jesus the Son of God, let us hold firmly to the faith we profess. For we do not have a high priest who is unable to empathize with our weaknesses, but we have one who has been tempted in every way, just as we are—yet he did not sin. Let us then approach God's throne of grace with confidence, so that we may receive mercy and find grace to help us in our time of need.

Hebrews 4:14-16 NIV

Regarding God, **hold firmly to what you believe and never allow anyone to sway your faith.** Do not be discouraged when you are tempted; Jesus faced temptation, too, and understands what you're going through. Because He did not give in, He is our High Priest forever. You can come with confidence straight into the Holy Place to freely receive God's mercy! The veil has been torn; *nothing* separates you from communion with your Creator.

It's in these times of fellowship that you experience His character. It's in these times of connection that He washes over you and brings healing to places that you did not even realize needed to be healed. It's in these times of communion that He whispers how much He loves you. Chains of sin you've struggled with for years will be broken. Scars of unforgiveness are erased while in His presence. Jesus longs to help you; there is no request too big or too small to bring to the Throne. **If it matters to you, it matters to Him.**

You don't even need to speak. **It isn't about your ability to express yourself; it is about His faithfulness.** His unceasing willingness to hear our cries and to stoop low and help us in our time of need.

The Word says that even when we are faithless, He remains faithful, because He cannot deny Himself. **He wants you to come as you are,** with all your brokenness and mess, and trust that He loves you extravagantly. Walk confidently into His presence, knowing He is waiting with anticipation to share time with you. You are so fiercely loved!

Today I pray,

Father God, I understand that You are my High Priest and forever, it is You that I will go to with all of my cares and concerns. I know that You suffered the same stuff I do, and You overcame it all. Enable me to overcome temptation and remind me to come to You to help me not sin. I love You! Amen.

Speak to Jesus All Day, Every Day

I have been crucified with Christ and I no longer live, but Christ lives in me. The life I now live in the body, I live by faith in the Son of God, who loved me and gave himself for me.
Galatians 2:20 NIV

Do you have a life verse? A Bible verse that sums you up completely when it comes to how you view Jesus as God and King and Supreme Ruler of your life?

When I was in my forties, Galatians 2:20 became my life verse. I had refreshed my relationship with the Lord and fallen into a habit of communicating with Him throughout the day, and more often, every hour. **I imagined He was with me, right beside me,** and I commented to Him on everything that happened, no matter how mundane.

I can't find my keys. *"Abba, I lost my keys again!"*

I stubbed my toe. *"Abba! Ow! That hurt!"*

I drive past a car accident. *"Abba Father, I pray for those people and First Responders in Jesus' name. Work Your will in their lives and may my prayer and worship set Your angels in motion to battle the enemies of God!"*

When we hear a truth such as Paul expresses here, **that he is so ONE with Jesus, that it's as if he was also crucified,** that everything he does and says is for Jesus, keeping in mind that our Savior suffered horrible torture so we may live forever in His presence, we realize that we can do that, too.

Paul was changed forever when he was saved in Messiah Jesus. So were we! **We're not the same people we were before we were saved.** Now, the Holy Spirit of God lives inside of us, continuously calling out to the Father, longing to be with Him, from within our hearts.

Begin tonight. Jesus' Spirit is inside you. Imagine He is physically beside you right now. Speak to Him. Make it a habit. Trust me, it is a glorious way to grow daily in your faith!

Tonight, I pray...

Father, I want to grow closer to You every day. I want to talk to You about everything. Show me how. Remind me that You're there when I forget, and enable me to get into a habit of thinking of You as right by my side. Thank You! Amen.

SHEEP TO THE PERFECT SHEPHERD

I am the good shepherd. The good shepherd
lays down his life for the sheep.

John 10:11 ESV

Jesus loves you so extravagantly that He lay down His life so you can live eternally with Him. He gave everything of Himself for you on the cross. Being the perfect shepherd, if you came up missing, He would leave the entire flock to come looking for you. **You are never, *ever*, for even for one moment, out of His sight.**

Think back over your life. Do you see His hand, even in the darkest of times, where He led and guided you in some way? The Word says that His sheep know His voice, they follow His voice, and He leads them out.[4] **When you feel as if you are in the deepest dungeon, Jesus leads you out.** Even if you don't realize that is what's happening, you end up safe in His sheep-pen because You belong to Him and your spirit heard His voice.

Jesus brightens the path home when you are lost. You may not see the way back clearly, but because Jesus is the Light and He came for you—his wandering sheep—you will have enough light to see.

Trust Him for every step; don't think ahead to tomorrow, next week, or next year. For now, just take the next step; allow Him to guide you. As you get closer to freedom, you will walk with more confidence at Jesus' side, able to see the light at the end of the dark path. You will be holding your head a higher, squaring your shoulders, because you realize you can trust Jesus. You know finally that He always has your best interest at heart.

Jesus knows what is best because He sees the end from the beginning. Rest assured, no matter what your circumstances look like or what the enemy whispers in your ear, all is well! Jesus is your good shepherd!

Today, I pray...

Father, I am that sheep who wanders away now and then. Thank You for always coming back for me. As I go about my day, I pray that You would help me stay mindful of Your will for my life. Help me remain focused on Your purposes and not my own. I want to be a good sheep for my perfect Shepherd. Amen.

The Worst Sinner in the World

The saying is trustworthy and deserving of full acceptance, that Christ Jesus came into the world to save sinners, of whom I am the foremost. But I received mercy for this reason, that in me, as the foremost, Jesus Christ might display his perfect patience as an example to those who were to believe in Him for eternal life.

1 Timothy 1: 15-16

Are you the worst sinner the world?

It may seem like a silly question but in this verse, Apostle Paul calls himself the chief of all sinners. He is saying that he is the worst sinner of all. How could that be? He's a pillar of our faith. A role model to all who call upon the name of the Lord Jesus! This is meaningful to believers because it reminds us to be humble.

Of all the people who followed Jesus, Paul labored mightily to further the Kingdom of God. If he considered himself the worst, each of us who tries to do *even a fraction of* what he accomplished in his day should understand that we are in no position to judge one another based upon perceived sin. Let us always consider we are *equally* unworthy of God's salvation, but **because of His great mercy, He is patient with us who believe on Him for eternal life.**

God resists the proud but gives grace to the humble. Remember to use your energy lifting each other up, not tearing them down. This is good for the entire Body!

Tonight, I pray...

Father, pride is a huge problem and I want to be more humble. Please cause me to hear You when You nudge me to dial back my pride. Please cause me to hear You when I have lifted myself above You in idolatry, thinking I deserve more than You've provided. I am at Your service. Please work Your perfect will in my life. Amen.

5

More Important than a Flower

"If God gives such attention to the appearance of wildflowers—most of which are never even seen—don't you think he'll attend to you, take pride in you, do his best for you? What I'm trying to do here is to get you to relax, to not be so preoccupied with getting, so you can respond to God's giving. People who don't know God and the way he works fuss over these things, but you know both God and how he works. Steep your life in God-reality, God-initiative, God-provisions. Don't worry about missing out. You'll find all your everyday human concerns will be met.

Matthew 6:30-33 TM

Have you ever seen a field of wildflowers? Wildflowers are beautiful in their natural environment without anyone taking care of them; that's because **God takes care of all creation. Even as precious as they are, they do not hold a candle to the way He feels about you,** His prized possession, His masterpiece. God delights in you and He loves to take care of you. He knows what you need even before you ask.

Let go and allow God to take control. Open your hand so He can place there all the good things He has stored up for you. Whether it is food for your family, clothes to wear, a car to drive, He knows, and if you will trust Him, and stop striving to fix everything yourself, He will provide what you need by His perfect wisdom.

God wants you to relax. Not only does worry affect your relationship with God, but it affects your health. Take a deep breath and let it go. Give it to God. It can be scary to relinquish control, but God is faithful. He will never let you down.

When you don't see your circumstances changing for a long time, trust Him all the more for His timing is perfect. He knows things we don't and He sees things beyond our comprehension. He is the Creator and He holds everything together.

God is moved with compassion for you. Don't stay frustrated and worried trying to figure out how to make something happen. Instead come to God, ask, and then trust that He hears your prayers. God will take complete and perfect care of you every time!

Today, I pray...

Father, help me let go of my worries. It seems the world is going crazy and I am afraid of losing everything I've worked for, everything I have done for my family and my church. Remind me that I never controlled any of this anyway. Remind me that You gave me everything I have and I did not earn it. Remind me that no matter what I see with my eyes, You hold me close and I am safe in Your care. Amen!

I Wanna Be A Veterinarian...

For I know the thoughts that I think toward you, says the LORD*, thoughts of peace and not of evil, to give you a future and a hope. Then you will call upon Me and go and pray to Me, and I will listen to you. And you will seek Me and find Me, when you search for Me with all your heart.*

Jeremiah 29:11 NIV

Do you believe that God has a plan for your life? When are young, our plans originate from parents, friends, authority figures, and/or the culture around us; such as, plans to go to college or trade school, plans to marry and have children, or maybe plans to travel or invest in a lifelong dream, etc. In hindsight, do you think **God steered your choices along the way** to put you where you are now?

When I was little, I wanted to be a veterinarian. I loved dogs and cats so much that I petted them everywhere I went. When I was fifteen, my dad took me to Auburn University Career Day where I signed up for "veterinarian." What I remember most about that day is seeing jars of preserved dog hearts riddled with worms. My career dreams changed that day. Instead, I pursued a degree in psychology. After graduation, I married my high school sweetheart, and started a family, becoming a stay-home mom.

All this time, I believed in God. Funny thing is, I don't remember ever asking God what He wanted me to do. As I matured in my faith, I began asking Him to lead me. **Looking back, I see He was nudging me all the way.** My ministry uses my psychology degree and marrying instead of going to Grad school set me on a path to always be able to work my business from home. God's plan *was and is* indeed perfect, and **I know I am where I'm supposed to be.** How about you? Let's line up our will with God's every day and see what amazing things He will do with us!

Tonight, I pray...

Father, I realize that You have a plan for my life. I want to be a willing partner in Your plan. I submit my will to Yours. Lead me down Your paths and show me how to live for You! In Jesus' name, amen.

6

UNIMAGINABLE DEPTHS OF GOD'S LOVE

This is real love—not that we loved God, but that He loved us and sent His Son as a sacrifice to take away our sins.
1 John 4:10 NLT

God doesn't love you because you love Him—He loves you because He *chose to do so.* Once you put your faith in Jesus, His love fixes upon you without end. Worldly love is based upon conditions, and if you fail to live up to those conditions, it can be taken away. This is not true with God's love.

God loved you before you were born. He loves you at your worst, and at your best. His love does not waiver, it is perfect and complete. God's love fights for you, and it is *fierce for you.*

Like a mighty ocean coming in waves, **God's love washes over you, a healing salve for all of your wounds.**

God's love is without ceasing, pursuing you even when you try to hide. When shame and guilt push you to flee, **God's love finds you, restores you, and redeems you.**

God's love stretched out its arms on a cross and died for you. *You* were the joy set before Him when He gave Himself as a willing sacrifice in our place. **Never doubt that you are extravagantly loved.** Allow yourself to believe this, to accept God's overwhelming, unquenchable, and unshakeable love!

Today, I pray...

Heavenly Father, thank You for loving me no matter what. I know Jesus died on the cross for my sins and I want to be with You for eternity. Day by day, teach me how to love like You do. Teach me how to be more like You every passing minute. In Jesus' name, Amen.

Make Me A Partner in God's Work

[Jesus said] *"Whoever desires to come after Me, let him deny himself, and take up his cross, and follow Me. For whoever desires to save his life will lose it, but whoever loses his life for My sake and the gospel's will save it.*

Mark 8:34-35 NKJV

How do I take up my cross? What in my life could I possibly consider equal to the cross on which Jesus was crucified? Most of us understand at a surface level that Jesus is saying believers must expect and accept all kinds of abuse from the world in His name. If we hold the testimony of Jesus Christ, we will offend unbelievers regularly enough, especially if we're vocal regarding our love for the Lord.

Jesus' cross was a heavy wooden beam that He was forced to carry to Golgotha that would also be a torture device that eventually held His dead flesh aloft. **How do I translate this symbology to my life?**

A believer's cross is the "burden" of knowing the Truth and being commanded to share it with the world. For most of us, it will not be a torture device in the way Jesus' was, but it is still often uncomfortable and can be frightening to bear it among worldly folks.

What's important to remember is that when we testify of our love of Jesus, He is right there with us, holding us close, and whispering in our ears how much He loves us. **Stand fast in your faith no matter what the enemy sends your way.**

Tonight, I pray...

Heavenly Father, teach me how to carry my cross in Your name. Teach me how to make my life about You and about performing Your will. Help me remember that the world hates me because it first hated You. I love you. Amen.

7

BELIEVE IN GOD'S PROMISES

And blessed is she who believed that there would be a fulfillment of what was spoken to her from the Lord.

Luke 1:45 ESV

In Luke Chapter One, the angel told Mary, a virgin, that she was going to become pregnant and give birth to Jesus. The angel assured her that she was blessed because she believed God would do what He said He would do. But virgin being found pregnant? This was an absolute impossibility! Yet, Mary didn't look at the situation and say there is no way this could happen. No, she took God at His word. **Is there a promise you believe God has made you, but you don't see any way it could happen?** These sorts of situations can be the perfect setup for God to perform a miracle!

God doesn't work according to human logic and when He makes a promise, He will fulfill it every single time. You don't have to know how or when the fulfillment will occur, you only trust it will happen. It is not in God's nature to make a promise and then not fulfill it; that would be cruel. No, our God is kind and compassionate, and loves to lavish His children with good gifts.

God will fulfill His promises to you. *Just believe.* Believe that He is good and wants to give you good things. Believe that it pleases Him to fulfill His promises. **What is impossible for man is possible with God.**

Don't try to figure out the details or tell God how you think He should do it. His resources are unlimited. God cannot be put in a box, and He has no boundaries.

God is 100% faithful. When you feel like giving up, hold on a little longer; it will happen just at the right time. **Dare to believe in God's providence.** You will not regret it.

Today, I pray...

Father, thank You for Your faithfulness and that Your love endures forever. I want to sing to You all day long about how wonderful You are. Today as I do my human work, please put Your song in my heart so I might find myself humming praise to You without even knowing I was in worship. I want to grow closer to You! Amen.

I REPENT, O LORD, I REPENT

For the Lord is our Judge, The Lord is our Lawgiver,
The Lord is our King; He will save us.

Isaiah 33:22 NJKV

Who likes to obey rules? Submit to another's will? Human nature resists the commands of outside controllers. Resistance to God's instruction (His Commandments) is the sin of rebellion. **Submission to God is the anchor of our faith in an unseen magistrate.** After all, He is our Judge. Did you realize that the first name of God in the Bible, Genesis 1:1, is JUDGE? "In the beginning, GOD…" which is the Hebrew word, "Elohim," meaning *judge, magistrate, ruler.* So, how important is obedience to God if He should reveal this as His first attribute?

Obedience is of utmost importance when we are growing our relationship with the Lord. Much of Paul's New Testament letters addressed this very thing. Just because he *could* sin did not mean he *should.* Paul taught that we are allowed to sin because we are saved, but we can't grow closer to God that way. In fact, an unrepentant life slowly separates us from God.

Picture that famous pictogram: God on one side, you on the other, and in between is a chasm labelled "sin." **Sin separates us from God.** So even though we are saved and will spend eternity with Him, 1 John reminds us that we are sinners and that we must repent[5]. Daily repentance is between you and Jesus alone.

Tonight, I pray...

Father, forgive me for my sins, every sin from the beginning of my life to now. Wash me clean with the blood of Jesus and teach me how to walk in Your Law, to understand Your Word, and give me a desire to seek Your will above all else. Amen.

LET MY FRUIT BE HIS FRUIT

"Abide in Me, and I in you. As the branch cannot bear fruit by itself,
unless it abides in the vine, neither can you,
unless you abide in Me."

John 15:4 ESV

Abide means to dwell, live in, or remain in. Jesus says for you to abide in Him, and He will abide in you. You are the branch, and He is the vine, and **you can do nothing apart from God.** Human effort accomplishes nothing. An apple tree does not strive and strain to produce an apple. The tree simply effortlessly produces. It is the same for you and me. We cannot do good things by merely *trying* to bear fruit. We must abide in Jesus, rest in Him, make our home in Him, and as a result, He causes us to bear good fruit.

Abiding in Him also means that you do not take credit for the good fruit you produce, rather Jesus receives all the glory and honor. **You bring glory to His name when you produce this abiding fruit.** Trust Jesus that He will do through you whatever needs to be done. When you are abiding in Him and everything is shaken, you will be able to survive the storm.

You may bend, but you will not break. The Vine will hold on to you when the winds and waves buffet. He is your protector, your defender, your place of refuge.

When you abide in Jesus, you also abide in the Father. The world is chaotic, but those who abide in Jesus are in a position of rest, in possession of the wisdom of God. Abiding in Him is a position of leaning on Him instead of trying to do everything alone. Today as you go about your day, make your home in Him and He will make your load easy and light.

Today, I pray...

Father, I sometimes forget that I need to remain in You, keep You on my mind, and turn to You for all matters, big and small. Today, please remind me as I go to abide in Your holy care. I don't want to a go a single day outside of Your protection. In Jesus' name, Amen.

DON'T GIVE UP ON ME, LORD

Seek the Lord while He may be found,
call upon Him while He is near.

Isaiah 55:6 NIV

Often when we come across this verse on social media, it's being used as a "threat." I've done it (and most of us have if we're in a ministering capacity), using Isaiah 55:6 as a warning, reminding folks that **God said, "I will not strive with man forever."**[6]

As valid as that interpretation is, consider this. "While God may be found," means literally, "until the events of Revelation when it becomes impossible to be saved." From now and into The Great Tribulation, unbelievers will have an opportunity to repent and be saved. Once Jesus returns to earth (the Second Coming), everyone alive will be judged on the status they have then.[7]

That seems like a long time off, so why worry about it now? There are some believers who depend on Jesus for salvation but refuse to submit to His teaching and live the moral, Gospel-led life that He commands.

That's no way to live the Christian life. The good works you do in Jesus' name and for God's kingdom do not affect your salvation, but they affect your spiritual growth, your relationship with the Father, your mortal friendships, and the "crowns" you receive at the judgment seat of Christ.[8] So let's seek God's presence now. Let's draw near to Him now.

Tonight, I pray...

"Father-God, I want to follow You, to do Your will, to perform good works that You have for me to do. Please cause Your will to be done in my life that I might please You. Teach me how to walk close to You every day. I don't want to walk a single step without You. Amen.

9

Only One Loves This Big

Because God's children are human beings—made of flesh and blood—the Son also became flesh and blood. For only as a human being could He die, and only by dying could He break the power of the devil, who had the power of death. Only in this way could He set free all who have lived their lives as slaves to the fear of dying.
Hebrews 2:14-15 NLT

Jesus became human, so He could die in human flesh, therefore breaking the power of the enemy. At the time, the devil had the power of death, but now everything has changed. Death has lost its sting. Jesus loved us so much that he suffered unimaginable torture to become a sacrifice for sin of all who will believe. **Who loves this big? Only Jesus!**

But there's more. **Not only did He die to save your soul; He died to deliver you from the fear of dying.** Death no longer has a hold over you. Jesus broke that hold, and now you have eternal life! When you take your final breath, you will go immediately to your forever home, the place that has been prepared for you.

How glorious will it be to see Jesus, the One who loves you beyond your comprehension, to behold His beauty, to have Him wrap you in His arms for a tangible hug. I believe when His love wraps itself around you, the feeling that you will feel will be greater than you could ever imagine.

You can have a portion of that feeling while still here on earth. You can feel His love for you, feel the warmth of that love wrapped around you. Even now, you can begin to live in eternity. True life begins the day you enter a relationship with Jesus. Take a moment, grow quiet, and sit in His presence. Calm your mind and don't rush it. Just rest in Him. Know you are fully loved and fully known right now and that you have nothing to fear, not even death. Hallelujah!

Today, I pray...

Father God, sometimes I am afraid to die. Will you remind me whenever that topic comes to my mind that You have conquered death. Remind me that I have nothing to fear, because no matter what this world might do to my physical body, my soul is safe in You. I do not need to fear death or anything else because I belong to You, and You are the perfect Father. I love You and I need You! Amen.

BLESSED MORE THAN I DESERVE

The Lord is compassionate and gracious, slow to anger, abounding in love. He will not always accuse, nor will he harbor his anger forever; **he does not treat us as our sins deserve or repay us according to our iniquities.** *For as high as the heavens are above the earth, so great is his love for those who fear him; as far as the east is from the west, so far has he removed our transgressions from us.*

Psalm 103:8-12 NIV

All of us sometimes feel dirty, unworthy, and ungrateful. We committed a sin (many times, we premeditated it, too!), and afterwards, we feel as if spiritual slime is oozing across our skin. While it's true we *will sin,* it is also true that embracing God's endless mercy and incredible patience with those who are saved does a lot to prove to God that we trust Him. **We trust His forgiveness is real and forever.** We acknowledge that He punishes us *much, much* less than we deserve. Give Him praise for that!

Along the same lines, think of how much He has blessed us much more than we deserve. I often pray saying, "Father, You have not dealt with me according to my sins. In Your mercy, You have not punished me according to what I deserve." Then I'll add, "But it is amazing how You have blessed me *so much more* than I deserve!"

Let's remember that because His mercy and loving-kindness lasts forever, **He forgives and thus erases our sin when we repent.** The Bible teaches us to not despise the chastisement of the Lord because He does this to burn off the dross in our spirits. More often than not, we repent before chastisement is required; that sin is erased forever, and we work to not sin again. Let's ask Him to help us *not sin!*

Tonight, I pray...

Father, I know I am a sinner, saved by Your grace. Convict me of sin *before* it happens, *after* I commit it, and remind me to repent. I won't wait for punishment to bring me to repentance—I will acknowledge my sin right away. I praise You for blessing me much more than I deserve!
Thank You!

10

JESUS IS MY MASTER

So if the Son sets you free, you will be free indeed.
John 8:36 ESV

There is a lot in this small verse. **Freedom is something we all long for.** You can search for it in many ways and many different places. You can experience what *feels* like freedom, but it turns out to be just another bondage formed in sin. This is why we need Jesus; there is no freedom like that which He gives.

Imagine it's like being in a prison created by our sin nature. Jesus holds the key to this jail cell and when He unlocks that door, you walk into true and lasting freedom. There is nothing and no one in this world that can do what Jesus can do. He is breathtaking and amazing and majestic, but He still comes to rescue you. You matter to Him. Your freedom matters to Him. He is the only way out.

Jesus is the Way, the Truth, and the Life. Galatians says it is for freedom that He has set you free. Do not allow anyone to put you back into slavery once you are freed by the Lord. When He sets you free, spread the news far and wide, telling all what Jesus did for you, and in turn giving them the hope of freedom as well.

Jesus wants to bring you freedom to enjoy life as you have never known. He wants to cause you to live in a wide-open space where you are not just kind of free, but abundantly and completely free. He wants to see you thrive, to see you sing and shout for joy. **Yes, life is hard, but when Jesus sets you free, you can dance in the midst of the storm.** Stand firm in the freedom He has given you, trusting He will keep you from harm. Hear Him say you are extravagantly loved and abundantly free!

Today, I pray...

Father, before I knew You, I only thought I was free. Now I know that Your sort of freedom is the one that lasts. I know I am safe with You and free from death, free from the power of satan, and I am free from the bonds of sin. May Your Holy Spirit nudge me when I need correction and keep teaching me that You love me extravagantly forever! Amen.

Let My Words Be Few

*Do not be quick with your mouth, do not be hasty in your heart to
utter anything before God. God is in heaven and you are on earth, so
let your words be few.*

Ecclesiastes 5:2 NIV

"Let your words be few," doesn't make much sense out of
context, because doesn't God want us to pray? But as with
every verse in the Bible, it is one teaching that fits into the
entire love letter from God. From beginning to end, the
words of the 66 Books of the Bible work together to express
God in a way Humans can comprehend. **The Bible never
contradicts itself,** and only seems to do so when verses are
taken out of the whole.

In Bible times and today, there are folks who think they can
use their tongue to get closer to God. Long prayers,
memorized tomes, even memorizing Scripture with the
wrong heart—these efforts are meaningless if you haven't
submitted your life to God and put your faith in the blood
Jesus.

**We can talk to God for hours upon hours once our heart
is connected to His.** You can wake up in the morning say,
"Hello, Father!" You can speak to Him all the way to the
shower, in the shower, on the ride to work, and throughout
your daily tasks. He loves that. This verse is not about this
connected conversation with the Lord that many of us enjoy
every day.

This is a warning to new and growing Christians who may have been brought up performing rituals to please a deity. That's not what our God wants now that Jesus has fulfilled His saving sacrifice. God wants to commune with us at a soul level, converse heart-to-heart. Long soliloquies have absolutely nothing to do with communicating with God.

Tonight, I pray...

Father-God, I pray I will speak to You all day, every day, straight from my heart. I know this is because Your spirit is within me talking to yourself! This existential, incomprehensible relationship is what we have together because I *know* Jesus died on the cross for my sins. I *know* He has been resurrected and sits right now at the right hand of God. Thank You for choosing me!
I love You, good night!

HE HELPS ME WHEN I'M HELPLESS

When he saw the crowds, he had compassion on them because they were confused and helpless, like sheep without a shepherd.
Matthew 9:36 NLT

Jesus wants to bring healing and rest to every area of your life. He doesn't want you to live a life of confusion and frustration. The devil is the author of confusion. Jesus brings peace and calm. You can trust in His love for you. His love is like a beautiful waterfall flowing continually over your life. Imagine standing under that waterfall and allowing it to wash over you.

Jesus is the good shepherd, and He takes good care of His sheep. **When you feel helpless and hopeless, Jesus steps in,** and He brings you help and hope. If you persevere, you will see His goodness in your life.

Jesus is the Lord of lords and the King of kings. He is not hard or harsh, He is not waiting to punish you. Jesus took your punishment upon Himself so that you would not have to suffer that punishment. **When no one else knows what you are going through, Jesus knows,** and He wants to help you.

He will not judge you or condemn you. His love outweighs anything you think you have done that disqualifies you. Even if the whole world condemns you, Jesus will accept you. When others call you unclean, Jesus comes to wash you as white as snow. He is your advocate. He fights for you. **His love is a river that never runs dry, and His arms are stretched wide.**

You are not forgotten. You are written on the palm of His hand. **When you are hurting, cry out to Him;** He will have compassion on you. You can square your shoulders and hold your head high, knowing You belong to God, a child of the Lord Most High!

Today, I pray...

Father, thank You for Your amazing compassion for me. When I am having the worst day of my life, thank You that I can come to You for comfort. You don't want to see me confused or dazed, but clear-headed and focused on God. Please work Your will in my life that I may become more like You daily. Amen.

5G is Melting My Brain

Come, behold the works of the LORD, Who has made desolations in the earth. He makes wars cease to the end of the earth; He breaks the bow and cuts the spear in two; He burns the chariot in the fire. **Be still, and know that I am God;** *I will be exalted among the nations, I will be exalted in the earth! The LORD of hosts is with us; The God of Jacob is our refuge. Selah*

Psalm 46: 8-11 NIV

Take a minute to read these three verses because what I'm about to say next is an explanation using the verse as it stands as well as in context.

It's hard to be still. It is hard to sit quietly. It's doubly difficult to calm our minds. **Jesus wants us to capture every thought for him,**[9] and Lord knows, our thoughts run rampant. Even though historically, it has always been a challenge to focus one's mind, those alive today are tasked more than ever because of modern technology. Not only do we have television, internet, and smart phones, we have radio waves in the form of microwaves all around us, constantly bombarding our brains.

Research 5G[10] (and don't use government-controlled search engines). 5G is a digital data-transferring microwave system stronger than any we've ever seen. Think of putting your hand in the microwave oven—yes, those waves. The next (and last?) level, 6G, is right around the corner.[11] **These waves assault electrical systems,** of which our brain and

43

nervous system identify as. This gives you a great excuse, beloved. It truly isn't your fault that your mind is racing.

Hope is not lost, of course! Jesus overcomes. When you want to speak to God and your brain is scampering with the troubles of the day or some personal excitement, pray, asking for His help. Try this…

Tonight, I pray...

Father, please calm my mind. In Jesus' name, block every intrusion of the enemy, including radio waves and microwaves that are assaulting me. Father, enable me to be still and focus on You. Enable me to find quiet in this chaos and let me hear You. I want to hear You. Amen.

To Be Holy and Blameless

*For God in all his fullness was pleased to live in Christ, and through Him, God reconciled everything to Himself. He made peace with everything in heaven and on earth by means of Christ's blood on the cross. This includes you who were once far away from God. You were His enemies, separated from Him by your evil thoughts and actions. Yet now He has reconciled you to Himself through the death of Christ in His physical body. As a result, He has brought you into His own presence, and **you are holy and blameless as you stand before Him without a single fault.***
Colossians 1:19-22 NLT

Jesus has made peace with everything in heaven and on earth through His blood on the cross. This means He has also made peace between you and God. Everyone has sinned at some point in their lives; Jesus is the only person who has ever been completely without sin.

Our sins separated us from God and made us His enemy, but we are now reconciled to God because of Jesus, the spotless Lamb. Now we can come boldly and with confidence into God's presence, without fear or consequences. No matter who you are or what you have done, if you have made Jesus the Lord of your life, you now stand before God completely clean, as white as snow.

This is something to celebrate! You can stand before a holy God without fear because Jesus has made us blameless. When God sees you, He doesn't remember your sin. He sees you the same way He sees Jesus: spotless, clean, pure, and righteous.

This has nothing to do with your good deeds or how well-behaved you have been. It is made possible by Jesus' perfect sacrifice on the cross. It was not a fair trade for Him, but He loves you so much! You don't have to work to pay Jesus back. You can't. It's impossible. **What Jesus did is finished once and for all, and it was enough for all time.**

Today, I pray...

Jesus, thank You! I know You were bruised and beaten, spit upon and rejected, tortured more than I can ever know. I know You did this because You love me. Because of Your sacrifice, I can know You. I am in awe of You, my Savior, and because of You, I can stand boldly in the presence of my God. Amen!

THE LONGEST PSALM

How sweet are Your words to my taste,
Sweeter than honey to my mouth!

Psalm 119:103 NKJV

Have you ever read this verse and not only thought it was corny, but you wished that it was true for you? Do you wish you could say that to God and be telling the truth? I'm here to tell you that you can.

To a young Christian it is corny, let's face it. But **the more you study God's word, the more you seek His will in your life** and the connection of your heart to His through Jesus, the more His word *is* sweet and like honey to your lips.

Psalm 119 is my choice for words of life that you can read aloud to the Lord every day, which greatly increases your connection with Him. Try it! Psalm 119 is *really, really* long, so feel free to read it to Him in little chunks. This small gesture of worship has made a beautiful impact on my relationship with Adonai and my love of His word.

This is how to begin your worshipful reading: *Father, please forgive me for my sins and I come before You now washed clean by the blood of Jesus.*

Now, imagine He is in the room with you, on His throne, and you before Him, worshipping. His glory is so bright that the light is alive, and it warms you down to your very atoms!

Begin to read Psalm 119, with your heart pointed toward Jesus. You can guarantee that your spirit is sitting in the throne room of God worshiping Him on high. **Bless the name of Jesus!**

Tonight, I pray...

Father, I want to read Your words back to You; let this be my worship to You. I am going to start with Psalm 119. Blessed are those whose ways are blameless, who walk according to the law of the Lord. Blessed are those who keep his statutes and seek Him with all their heart...

13

I Want to Be a Mary

"There is only one thing worth being concerned about. Mary has discovered it, and it will not be taken away from her."
Luke 10:42 NLT

So many things seek your attention throughout the day. Some things are good, and some, not so good. **In today's fast-paced world, it is hard to focus on God.** We must balance jobs and families, and if we have kids and they are involved in things, we must transport them to their events. We are pulled in so many different directions through myriads of voices that swirl around us every moment of every day.

When the Bible tells of Martha and Mary, Lazarus's sisters, we learn that while Martha made herself busy preparing food and serving everyone, her sister sat at the feet of Jesus, listening to Him teach. **Martha became aggravated that Jesus would not send Mary to help her.**

Instead, Jesus said Mary had discovered the one thing that was worth being concerned about: being in Jesus' presence, taking in His word.

Jesus said that these things would not be taken away from Mary because they were *eternal things*. What does that mean to us today? Everything around us can be shaken at any moment, **but Jesus is unshakeable.** It is important to take care of your families and your responsibilities, but you cannot allow those temporary things to cause you to miss out on the eternal things, such as the most important thing of all—your relationship with Jesus.

If you focus on Him, everything else will fall into place. Jesus must be your first thing. Your first love, above even your spouse and your children. King David said there was one thing he sought, and that was to dwell in the house of the Lord all the days of his life, **to be in his presence.**

Today, I pray...

Father, King David was described as a man after God's own heart. Please enable me to make time to spend with You. I want to develop a habit of praying, singing, worshipping, and simply basking in Your presence every day. I want to taste and see that God is good! Father, make me more like Jesus every day. Amen.

Quench My Thirst

O God, You are my God; early will I seek You; my soul thirsts for You; my flesh longs for You in a dry and thirsty land where there is no water.

Psalm 63:1 NIV

This is a verse about prayer. How is that so? When the Psalmist was saying these words to God, he was pouring out his love. He understood that God's majesty is beyond comprehension. Say this verse aloud to God, tell your own ears, announce it to any spirits in the room with you right now. Say it out loud! You will also sense the hugeness of our Father, and you will want to read more. **You will thirst for more.**

The day is hectic and filled with strife, trouble, tribulation, and insult. Put this verse (or any favorite Psalm) at your bedside so as you go to sleep each night you can pray to God *His own words.* **You will sleep in His peace.** Try it and see!

Tonight, I pray...

Father, I am so busy and overwhelmed with everything I'm supposed to do and that I have committed to doing for the world and my ministry that I sometimes forget to just read Your words back to you with a heart of praise and worship. Remind me to do this each night and fill me with Your peace. Fill me with Your shalom when I rise. Thank You, Father, for a good night's rest and a vibrant morning that I may attack the world and perform Your will. In Jesus' name, amen.

GOD LOVED ME FROM THE BEGINNING

How blessed is God! And what a blessing He is! He's the Father of our Master, Jesus Christ, and takes us to the high places of blessing in Him. Long before He laid down earth's foundations, He had us in mind, had settled on us as the focus of His love, to be made whole and holy by His love. Long, long ago, He decided to adopt us into His family through Jesus Christ. (What pleasure He took in planning this!) He wanted us to enter into the celebration of His lavish gift-giving by the hand of His beloved Son.

Ephesians 1:3-6 TM

Before God flung the stars in the sky, before He spoke light into existence, before He made the fish of the sea or the animals on the land, He thought of you. **You are and always have been the focus of His love.**

God's love pours out on you in many different ways. Sometimes it is through the smile of a passerby. It may be through the laughter of a child. Sometimes it comes from a kind word or a gift from someone you love. Sometimes God sends His love through a stranger. **No matter how He sends it, He is continually pouring His love out on you.**

Nothing in this world except the love of God can make you whole. You are made *holy* by His love poured out on a cross for you. That blood that made you brand new the moment you believed. His blood is the evidence of His love for you. He decided He wanted you. He chose you.

God took great pleasure in planning this. Just as families plan for a new child, they get excited about the child coming home. There is so much anticipation and excitement. He also takes pleasure in lavishing His gifts on His children. He wants you to come to Him as a child would come to a parent and have confidence in asking Him for the things you want and need. It is a celebration for Him. If you are a parent, you know the feeling of buying your child a gift you know they wanted, and the excitement and anticipation of them opening that gift are so great. A good parent loves to give their children good gifts. This is how your Father is with you!

Today, I pray...

Father, I know there's nothing I can do to earn Your love. Thank You that You loved me first. I know the blood of Jesus allows me to have a relationship with You. I believe! Teach me to be a better child to my Father in heaven. I want to be like You. In Jesus' name, amen.

I will Rejoice No Matter What

Rejoice in the Lord always. I will say it again: Rejoice!

Philippians 4:4 NIV

Something terrible has happened in the world today. Something tragic has happened in your family this week. Something horrible and offensive and insulting happened to you only an hour ago. No matter—**the Lord says, rejoice!**

Rejoicing in times of trouble is a main theme in the New Testament. To a new Christian, it seems senseless and maybe even a little cruel for God to expect us to dance in the storms, but this is exactly what He expects His called-out ones to do. **Your joy in dark times is proof of your faith in God's promises**—this blesses His heart.

Can you rejoice when a loved one has perished at a young age? When a storm destroys homes across the state? When an accident takes the lives of a hundred innocents? You may read Philippians 4:4 in these times and think, "There's no way He meant rejoice ALWAYS…" But He did. Who brings calamity? God. **Nothing happens without His approval.** It is a hard teaching, but it is easy to understand and easy to ask God for help with.

Tonight, I pray...

Father, help me rejoice! I cannot fathom how I can be
happy when the world is so evil. But You know all things
and You will show me how to rejoice in the Lord, no matter
what I see with my eyes. I rejoice that I know I am saved,
and I rejoice that You are in control of every situation. I
rejoice because you said You bring peace and calamities.
You will teach me how to rejoice always in the Lord's
promises. Amen.

15

OUT OF THE SHADOWS INTO THE LIGHT

Everything was created through Him; nothing—not one thing!—came into being without Him. What came into existence was Life, and the Life was Light to live by. The Life-Light blazed out of the darkness; the darkness couldn't put it out.

John 1:3-5 TM

Jesus is amazing. He is breathtaking. He calls things into existence that do not exist. He was there when everything was created. Not one thing was created without Him, including you. He can change atoms and molecules if He needs to. All He has to do is speak and things are created or rearranged. Jesus is Life, and He is Light!

We can walk in His light when we live a life with Him. He shines brightly in the darkness, and there is no darkness in all of hell that can ever extinguish the Light! He puts His light in you, and you begin to shine brightly for Him. His beautiful, astonishing, breathtaking life and light lives in and through you, and it shines for the whole world to see.

Don't be afraid to shine, for the very One who created everything and holds everything together is the One who lives in you! Allow His brightness to beam through every single cell of your body. It brings Light and Life to those who are hiding in the darkness. This Light is the most powerful light there is. Don't let others tell you to dim your light, and when they do, just let it cause you to shine even brighter, because it isn't you that shines, it is Jesus shining through you.

Darkness runs from this Light. The enemy recognizes this Light in your life and doesn't want you to realize who you are in Jesus. Satan will try to cause you to keep your head down so no one can see the Light in you. But you were created to shine and you will fulfill that purpose! Shame causes you to want to stay in the shadows, to shrink back in obscurity, but Jesus defeated shame and stripped it of its power to harm. You no longer need to lurk in the shadows. You are called a child of the Light. **Step out of the shadows, in Jesus' mighty name.**

Today, I pray...

Father in heaven, You have called me to live free, to shine the Light of Jesus always. Jesus lights my path everywhere I go. Father, show me how to leave a legacy of Light and Life to those around me every day. Amen.

EYES DON'T SEE WHAT MY HEART KNOWS

Be anxious for nothing, but in everything by prayer and supplication, with thanksgiving, let your requests be made known to God; and the peace of God, which surpasses all understanding, will guard your hearts and minds through Christ Jesus.

Philippians 4: 6-7 NKJV

"Be anxious for nothing." **Those four words of Scripture need no explanation.** Paul says as clearly as possible that because of Jesus and His promises, because Scripture from beginning to end is trustworthy and true, we have no reason to be afraid.

Prayer, supplication, and giving God thanks for His providence all help us to discern God's presence and protection in rough times. Your constant turning to Him when the world is crashing around you clears your mind and protects you from the spirit of fear.

I have periods in my life when things are falling apart and I am rejoicing in the Lord despite what I see with my eyes. Sometimes, onlookers among family and friends despise me for it. If we seem calm when chaos surrounds us, people can become offended at your peace. To prevent others from stumbling in these times, you can tamp down your joy and hold the praise and worship in your heart that God has the situation well in hand.

Tonight, I pray...

Father, remind me to seek You when things get hairy in my life. I will come to You with my prayer requests, my worries, and my praise every day and every night. Show me how to rejoice in the dark times. I love You and I need You! Amen.

16

Everlasting Love

And I am convinced that nothing can ever separate us from God's love. Neither death nor life, neither angels nor demons, neither our fears for today nor our worries about tomorrow—not even the powers of hell can separate us from God's love. No power in the sky above or in the earth below—indeed, nothing in all creation will ever be able to separate us from the love of God that is revealed in Christ Jesus our Lord.
Romans 8:38-39 NLT

There is no person on earth and no demon in hell that can come between you and God's love. Add to that, your doubts, fears, and anxieties can never separate you from God's love. NOTHING, **absolutely nothing can separate you from the love of God for you.**

You didn't earn God's love, and you can't lose it. He can never love you more than He does right now, and He can never love you less. This magnificent, ever-flowing, never-ending love of God was revealed in the fact that He gave His one and only Son to die for you. If you ever begin to doubt that you are loved, **fix your eyes on the cross.**

When you behold the cross, you bring to remembrance the stripes that were placed on Jesus's back, the nails that were put in His hands and feet, the crown of thorns that was placed on His head, and the sword that pierced His side, you realize there is no greater love than that. Not because we loved Him, but because He loved us! **This love is the most powerful force on earth.** It can turn a heart of stone into a heart of flesh. It can cause blind eyes to see and the lame to walk. It can bind up broken hearts and put families back together.

The perfect love of Jesus can break any addiction. It drives out fear. It washes away shame. It makes the unclean clean again. It is a firm foundation under your feet. You can build your life on it and know it will never crumble. God loves you so much! He doesn't want you to just know about His love; He wants you to experience it yourself. If you ask, He will give you a revelation of His love that will change your life forever. There is and never will be a love that is greater than the love your God has for you.

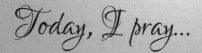

Today, I pray...

Father, thank You that Your love chases me down. Your love is everlasting and You will hold me close forever so matter what. Please continue to teach me how to serve You. I want to do Your will. I am Your servant. Amen.

GOD'S ARROW IN MY HEART

Blessed is the man who walks not in the counsel of the ungodly,
Nor stands in the path of sinners, nor sits in the seat of the scornful;
but his delight is in the law of the Lord, and in His law he meditates
day and night.

Psalm 1:1-2 NKJV

Do you delight in the "law" of the Lord? This is one time when it would be helpful to have a concordance to translate the word "law," to help us understand the context.

In English, "the law" brings to mind police officers, judges, and attorneys, and to an extent, that's what it means here as well. But in a greater and more important sense, it means "the entire way of God".

The word "Law" used here is in Hebrew, "Torah" (pronounced, *tore* – **ah** with accent on the second syllable). This word means, *"Law, rule, commandment, with an indication of an arrow, as in a word from God that goes right into your heart."* **God wants His *Torah* to pierce your heart.**

King David said his delight is in reading God's word and he meditates in it day and night. Even the word "meditate" brings up images that we have in the English language that aren't exactly what the Hebrew means. It means to the believer that **God wants us to keep His Word on our minds, day and night.**

When we arise, when we go about our day, and when we fall asleep, we can ponder the meaning and the enormity of God's word. Let's do that ourselves!

Tonight, I pray...

Father, forgive me for being busy. Forgive me for being scattered. I want to study Your *Torah*, Your scriptures, every day. And on days that the world prevents me from opening my Bible, may Your Holy Spirit bring it to my thoughts that I may meditate on it even when there's no Bible around. Father, make me a walking living Bible to the glory of Jesus Christ. Thank You! Amen.

17

Jesus is Willing

Suddenly, a man with leprosy approached Him and knelt before Him. "Lord," the man said, "if You are willing, You can heal me and make me clean." Jesus reached out and touched him. "I am willing," He said. "Be healed!" And instantly the leprosy disappeared.

Matthew 8:2-3 NLT

Have you ever wondered if Jesus was willing? This man was a leper, which meant he would have been exiled out of the town to a leper colony. No one would dare to touch a leper or even be near a leper at this time. It took a lot of courage for this man to come close to ask Jesus for healing. He even wondered if the Lord would even be interested in healing his condition.

Jesus had tremendous compassion for this man and didn't tell the man to go away. He wasn't afraid for the leper to touch Him either. In fact, Jesus touched the man Himself in the process of removing the illness. Imagine what that gesture meant to those watching on!

Sometimes in our lives, we, like the leper, *know* Jesus can heal us, but we wonder if He will. It is true that we can't know why God heals some and not others, but we can be certain that Jesus loves us, and that He is no respecter of persons. He knows things we don't know and sees things we cannot see. He sees the end from the beginning. We must trust the outcome to Him.

God has our absolute best interests at heart in everything that He does. His compassion for you moves Him to work on your behalf. Always believe for the absolute best, but even if it doesn't happen, know that it isn't because you aren't loved, or because you have failed somehow, or you have gone too far for Jesus to hear your prayer. **It doesn't matter what you have done or how deep the pit of sin you find yourself in; Jesus always is moved with compassion for you.**

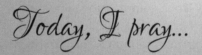

Father, thank You that Your heart is always toward me, that my condition never revolts You. Nothing in my life surprises You. You knew me before I took my first breath and You loved me. Thank You for your lovingkindness! You restore my soul! Amen.

Don't Speak to Angels

*The angel of the Lord encamps all around those who fear Him,
and delivers them.*

Psalm 34:7 NIV

Gina and I entitled this devotional *Wrapped in the Light* for the specific purpose of sharing that sensation of being wrapped up in the love of Jesus Christ. The experience of Almighty **God on His throne, hugging us with the invisible bonds of His enormous love.**

This verse reminds us that the angel of God is constantly with us. We have angels assigned to us from birth[12] who are constantly with us and in the presence of God. Picture it like this, an angel is a spirit, not bound by flesh, and he can watch over us and simultaneously be in the throne room with God. As if standing on a doorway threshold, the angel can see both rooms at once! **This is so our "guardian" angel(s) can guide us according to the will of God.**

God allows us to "see" the angels in our mind's eye. Try it now. Imagine an angel in the room with you, not to worship, but just to know he is there. **Never speak to angels; instead, thank God that He provides them!** Use this knowledge to send praise and thanks to the Most High, that even though we live in a fallen world, God provides these "helpers" all along the way. Right now, as you read this devotion, and you have been born again in Jesus Christ, there is *definitely* one or more angels are in the room with you. Hallelujah!

Tonight, I pray...

Father, I believe You! I believe You have set an angel to watch over me and thank You for that. I won't talk to him and I won't worship him, but I will thank You for and give You all glory and all praise. I will say with my mouth that You are God and You are King and that You protect those who belong to You! You will work Your will in my life! I love You! Good night.

I SHALL NOT WORRY

Do not fret or have any anxiety about anything, but in every circumstance and in everything, by prayer and petition (definite requests), with thanksgiving, continue to make your wants known to God. And God's peace [shall be yours, that tranquil state of a soul assured of its salvation through Christ, and so fearing nothing from God and being content with its earthly lot of whatever sort that is, that peace] which transcends all understanding shall garrison and mount guard over your hearts and minds in Christ Jesus.
Philippians 4:6-7 AMPC

God does not want us to worry about anything, instead, He tells us to pray about *everything,* and to *continue* to pray. There is no worry too big or too small to bring to His attention. **He cares about everything that concerns you.**

Instead of allowing yourself to worry, turn those worries into prayers and petitions. Be specific in your prayers. Pour your heart out to God. He can handle anything you want to tell Him. He already knows everything about you anyway. Once you turn that worry and anxiety into prayer, then you can rest and leave it with God, knowing He cares about every detail of your life, and He will always do what is best for you in every situation.

When you give it all to Him, you can feel content and know that He is working on your behalf even when you don't see the evidence of it yet. God then gives you His peace that guards your heart and your mind in Christ Jesus. Allow the Prince of Peace to enter your situation. You will have the kind of peace that causes you to rest your head on your pillow at night and not worry about how things will turn out because you trust in the faithfulness of God. When the world encounters chaos, the first reaction is to freak out, but with Jesus, you can show them what true peace looks like. You can show them how to *truly rest* because the One you trust in is bigger than anything you can face.

God never sleeps nor slumbers. He is constantly looking out for you, protecting you, bringing the right people at the right time into your situation. He opens doors that no man can open and closes doors to protect you from walking through them. Never feel like your concerns do not matter to God. He loves you and wants to help you. He wants you to invite Him into your situation.

Today, I pray...

Father, allow Your peace to wash over me, please take control of my circumstances. I release all my worries to you so I may rest in Your care. I know everything is going to be all right because I belong to You. Amen.

I Am Not Afraid

The Lord is my light and my salvation;
whom shall I fear? *The Lord is the strength of my life; of whom*
shall I be afraid? When the wicked came against me to eat up my
flesh, my enemies and foes, they stumbled and fell. Though an army
may encamp against me, my heart shall not fear; though war may rise
against me, in this I will be confident.
Psalm 27:1-3 NKJV

There are multiple Bible verses regarding how we are not to be afraid because we belong to the Lord. This one, in particular, precursors this sentiment, asserting that God is our light and my salvation. Why put the thoughts in that order? Because God wants us to know *because* He has saved our souls from hell, we should not fear anything that happens to our flesh. In other words, **no matter what happens on earth, we will spend eternity with Jesus.**

When we're young, we don't think much about death and dying, but as we age, it's on our minds quite a bit. David says in this Psalm, "my heart shall not fear even if war rises up against me."

We are in some very dark days right now in 2021 and it *does* feel as if war is rising up around believers. When we stand for what we believe in and are thusly attacked, it can be scary. The beautiful thing about the way God has this set up is that it will always be fruitful. God's word will never return void— it will accomplish its work every time. **Let us pray for God to give us the courage in Him and His promises that we won't be afraid.**

Tonight, I pray...

Father, I want to be brave. I want to not fear the wicked
and the enemy always out to get me, always trying to kill
me. Please enable me to me to trust Your promises. Show
me with Your Holy Spirit that I may have peace in You all
day long and all night. That no matter what arises in my
life, fill me up with courage and faith. Cause me to believe
that I am safe no matter what happens to my body. I know
I am safe because I belong to You!

19

I AM GOD'S PRIZED POSSESSION

It's in Christ that we find out who we are and what we are living for.
Long before we first heard of Christ and got our hopes up, He had
His eye on us, had designs on us for glorious living, part of the overall
purpose He is working out in everything and everyone.
Ephesians 1:11-12 TM

Jesus loves to whisper His love over you. He loves to tell you who you are and, Whose you are. He speaks words of peace and rest over you. **Before you ever thought about Jesus, He already knew you**.

He knew you before He formed you in your mother's womb. Before you were born, He set you apart. You are His beloved, chosen, called, hand-picked. **You are the apple of His eye, His prized possession.** He calls you a masterpiece, a work of art. You are His child, and He lavishes you with His love.

Jesus has a purpose for your life, a destiny for you to fulfill. **There is something for you to do that no one else can,** people for you to reach that no one else can reach in a way you can. He knit you together the way you are for a reason, from the color of your hair and eyes to your personality and the sound of your voice. You have value and worth, and your life matters.

God has specific blueprints for your life. He has already recorded every day of your life. You have an incredible story to tell that no one else can tell. God wants you to be a beacon of hope and light to those around you. You are irreplaceable.

Your voice matters and needs to be heard. Never let anyone shut down your voice. Jesus smiles when He sees you. He is proud of you and pleased with you. He hasn't chosen you because you are intelligent or well educated, or wealthy, or famous. He has chosen you because He loves you, and He wants you to be a part of what He is doing in His Kingdom.

Seek Him and ask Him to reveal your purpose. He may not show you all at once, but step by step, He will guide you and unfold His plans before you. **Never compare yourself to anyone else, you are co-laborers, not competitors.** Walk out into this world and shine for Jesus like no one else can.

Today, I pray...

Hallelujah, Father, that You chose me! Before I was even born, You had a special job for me alone. I want to perform Your will! Please show me the way. I ask for the wisdom and understanding of God, and all the good gifts that the Spirit wants to bestow so I can fulfill my tasks. I will perform Your will because I love You. Thank You for Jesus. Amen!

WASHING DISHES FOR JESUS

Bondservants, obey in all things your masters according to the flesh, not with eyeservice, as men-pleasers, but in sincerity of heart, fearing God. And **whatever you do, do it heartily, as to the Lord** *and not to men, knowing that from the Lord you will receive the reward of the inheritance; for you serve the Lord Christ.*
Colossians 3:23

Do everything as if you're doing it for Jesus. This verse struck me from the moment I first read it. The thought was born in my spirit right then was that I could do 100% of my life for Jesus. What an amazing thought! Washing dishes, exercising, playing with the kids, I could do all of these things as if Jesus had asked me to do them. As you can imagine, this made every task more worthwhile and removed the grumbling some jobs elicited.

There are plenty of things we *don't want to do* and there are things we wish we didn't *have to do*. But if you imagine Jesus made the request, you can hop on it with a smile knowing this brings honor to the Lord. It also draws you closer to Him because of your obedience!

Tonight, I pray...

Dear heavenly Father, forgive me for so many times I grumble when I'm supposed to be doing stuff for you or for the world. Please make my heart like Yours, so I will do all things with You in mind. That I will perform tasks as if You had asked me to do them. The joy in my heart that I have in Your mercy and grace is overflowing. Father, cause me to do Your will with joy! Thank You!

20

UNTO TO US A SON IS BORN

*For to us a Child is born, to us a Son is given; and the government
shall be upon His shoulder, and His name shall be called
Wonderful Counselor, Mighty God, Everlasting Father,
Prince of Peace.*

Isaiah 9:6 ESV

Jesus is so beautiful! He is so majestic. He is the Lord of lords and the King of kings. He stepped down from heaven to be born as a man so He could save you. He did this because of God's great love for you.

No one can love you that way that Jesus can. There is just something about His name. *Jesus*… it is like honey on your lips. It can break every chain. It sends demons to flight. The name of Jesus can heal the sick and mend a broken heart. The name of Jesus has power and majesty. All heaven and earth proclaim His name!

One day, every knee will bow, and every tongue will confess that Jesus Christ is Lord! **He is holy and perfect,** yet He took upon Himself all our sins and gave us His righteousness. He is called *Wonderful Counselor* because He guides us when we are broken and wounded. He is better than any mortal therapists.

Jesus is the Everlasting Father. His kingdom has no end. He was, He is, and He is to come. He is the Great I AM. He is kind and compassionate to you as your Father. He is a jealous Father who will not share you with others.

Jesus is the Prince of Peace. He calms your fears and anxieties. He gives you peace that goes way beyond our understanding. His peace guards you and holds you. May all earth glorify Him and make His name famous above all. He is the Darling of Heaven, The Lamb of God, The Bright, and Morning Star. Even the rocks and trees cry out in praise at His name. All other kings, and kingdoms will pass away, but Jesus will remain eternal. Hallelujah!

Today, I pray...

Heavenly Father, thank You for sending Jesus. We love the Nativity story, the thought of Jesus as an infant, born to a virgin. But even more than that, we love how He loves us and gave His life so we could all be saved. You are my Wonderful Counselor, Almighty God, Everlasting Father, my Prince of Peace. Amen.

HELP ME STOP COMPLAINING

Do all things without complaining and disputing, that you may become blameless and harmless, children of God without fault in the midst of a crooked and perverse generation, among whom you shine as lights in the world...

Philippians 2:14-15a NKJV

Wahh. Wahh. Wahh. **Do you ever feel guilty when you complain?** I do. This verse comes to my mind always accompanied with the story of Job. No matter how hard my life might be, it will never be as difficult as that of Job.

So how do we combat this? As always, with prayer. When we find ourselves complaining, stop and thank God for our circumstances. Thank God that He is in control of today, yesterday, and tomorrow. **Thank Him that He has a plan, and His will *will* be performed.**

It's a sign of maturity to be able to resist complaining when the world says you have every right to. In these times, when things aren't going your way, use this opportunity to draw closer to Jesus. Explain your situation to Him and ask Him to help you. Then trust that He will. **Trust that He will make things right according to His will.**

Tonight, I pray...

Dear Father, I'm sorry for complaining and thank You for bringing it to my attention. Please remind me that no matter what is going on in my life, You have a plan for me and I can trust it wholeheartedly. Please remind me that no matter what I see with my eyes, You are working Your perfect will in my life. I submit to You, and I want to be with You forever. I bless You in the name of Jesus! Amen.

LEARNING FROM THOMAS

Now Thomas, one of the twelve, called the Twin was not with them when Jesus came. So the other disciples told him, "We have seen the Lord." But he said to them, "Unless I see in His hands the mark of the nails, and place my finger into the mark of the nails, and place my hand into His side, I will never believe."
Eight days later, his disciples were inside again, and Thomas was with them. Although the doors were locked, Jesus came and stood among them and said, "Peace be with you." Then He said to Thomas, "Put your finger here, and see My hands; and put out your hand, and place it in My side. Do not disbelieve, but believe."
Thomas answered Him, "My Lord and my God!"
Jesus said to him, "Have you believed because you have seen Me? Blessed are those who have not seen and yet have believed."
John 20:24-29 ESV

I'm so glad God included Thomas in the Bible. Thomas shows us that God loves us and is patient with us even when we have doubts. Jesus didn't get mad at Thomas or kick him off the disciple team because he doubted. No, Jesus was kind and willing to provide proof that it was Him.

Jesus is okay with your doubts. It doesn't scare Him or worry Him when you doubt. Remember, the Bible tells us that Jesus felt everything we feel, so I am sure He felt doubt at some point in His journey on earth. Doubt doesn't mean you have a lack of faith. Remember that your faith is not in the thing you are asking for; your faith is in the Person of Jesus Christ.

The Bible tells us that God's ways are perfect and that all His promises prove true. Don't allow yourself to let guilt and condemnation come upon you just because you may have a moment of doubt. Go to God and ask Him for help with your doubt. Ask Him for confirmation of what He has spoken over you.

Gideon asked God for proof twice when He put out the fleece. He knew that what He was telling Gideon was beyond man's comprehension. Thus, He did what Gideon asked and gave Him the confirmation He needed. **Jesus says that you are already blessed if you believe in Him.** Thomas believed in Jesus because he saw Him, but when you believe in Jesus without having seen Him, you reveal that you have faith. Remember, Romans 8:1 says, *"There is now, therefore, no condemnation for those who are in Christ Jesus."* Give yourself a break and invite Jesus to help you with your doubt. He will graciously help you.

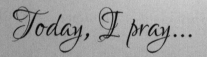

Today, I pray...

Father, forgive me for my doubt. Plant Your seed of faith within me and cause that seed to grow and grow and grow. I want my faith to be so huge that people can see it in my very countenance! I know You will do this if I ask, and so I do. Grow my faith! In Jesus' name, amen.

I WILL TREMBLE WITH HOLY FEAR

Therefore, my beloved, as you have always obeyed, not as in my
presence only, but now much more in my absence, **work out your**
own salvation with fear and trembling; *for it is God who*
works in you both to will and to do
for His good pleasure.
Philippians 2:12-13 NKJV

How in the world can this be a comforting verse? Work
out my salvation with fear and trembling? When I first read
this Bible verse, it struck me as being of the utmost
importance in the way I relate to the people around me. No
matter what I see with my eyes, I can't know what is going
on in another person's heart. I can't know at a glance what
anyone's relationship is with Jesus. That's why **this scripture**
reminds us that every individual is continually working
to serve (or avoid serving) the Creator.

Humans are born to parents, they usually live in some sort
of group—a family or community—and in a larger sense, in
a state or nation. But also (and most importantly) each man,
woman, and child is an individual. It is as an individual that
each of us make the choice to either spend eternity with Jesus
or be cast into hell upon our physical death.

I think this verse gives us comfort because right now as you
read this, you are communicating with the Father. **We love**
God with fear and trembling in the sense of holy fear

and a holy trembling. Imagine standing before the Creator of the universe. Your knees buckle, your jaw drops. There is no question, humans will not be able to stand before God. He is utter majesty, and the magnitude of his glory will bring all of us to our knees. Let's thank God for that and pray for all those who are struggling right now to know the peace of God.

Tonight, I pray...

Father, thank You for drawing me to You. And thank You, Lord, that You chose me. Please remind me every day that there are people struggling all around me, and that I can't see what stresses are in their lives. I can't see their relationship with You. But You see their hearts and You know them. Remind me to pray for these people and be compassionate—to see past what I see with my human eyes. I pray Jesus' holy name for Your will to be done in my life and in the life of every believer, and it is as it is in heaven. I love You! Amen

I WILL LEAP WITH JOY

But for you who fear my name, the Sun of Righteousness will rise with healing in His wings. And you will go free, leaping with joy like calves let out to pasture.

Malachi 4:2 NLT

When we think of the *fear of the Lord*, sometimes we picture someone who we should be afraid of, someone who is out to get us, waiting to punish us for everything we do wrong. This causes you to shrink back from God instead of running to Him. **The *fear of the Lord* is to stand in awe of Him,** to bow down to Him, give Him your worship because He deserves it. You can freely go to Him and not shrink back. You understand that He is Holy and Majestic, but at the same time, He is kind and gentle. He longs for you to come to Him with your requests. He longs to be good to you. He longs to heal you.

Jesus is the healer, the Sun of Righteousness. Demons must bow in His presence. When Jesus walks into your life, you will never be the same. He heals your spirit, your mind, your emotions, and your body. Sometimes we do not fully experience all our healing this side of heaven, but we will experience it. He can go to the deepest of wounds and the darkest of places in your life and bring healing if you invite

Him in. He knows and sees the places and the things inside you that you hide from everyone else. He will not be hard and harsh in His healing, but He will be gentle and allow you to heal at your own pace.

Jesus will walk with you all the way to freedom. He will never abandon you in your time of need. You can be completely honest and transparent with Him and confess the things that plague your mind. **He will sit with you while you cry and allow you to scream when you are angry.** None of this changes His affections for you. He will pour His healing oil over your life, and just like a caterpillar goes into a cocoon and emerges as a beautiful butterfly, Jesus will wrap you in His love and bring transformation from the inside out.

Today, I pray...

Dear Jesus, thank You that You don't do things halfway. You fill me with unspeakable joy! Thank You for my healing, today, tomorrow, and forever.
Thank You for loving me!

Asking for Wisdom in the Storm

Blessed be the God and Father of our Lord Jesus Christ, the Father of mercies and God of all comfort, who comforts us in all our tribulation, that we may be able to comfort those who are in any trouble, with the comfort with which we ourselves are comforted by God.

2 Corinthians. 1:3-4 NKJV

We created this devotional because we wanted to share the feeling of an *embrace* that we as believers feel whenever we worship, pray, and communicate with God. In this passage, He reveals that we will struggle, **we will have tribulation, but He will be there to comfort us.**

Let us always remember to acknowledge God's willingness to comfort us when we're upset. Let's ask Him to remind us that He does these things for His purpose. If any of us lacks wisdom, **ask God for wisdom.** He gives to all liberally and without reproach.[13]

Tonight, I pray...

Dear Father, I'm hurting. I'm suffering, and nothing I do
seems to help. I know that Your word says that You will
comfort me, so I ask for that right now in Jesus' name.
Father, please take away this pain. Remind me that this is
what You want, that You want to comfort me right now.
Turn my heart to You all the more. And thank You that you
watch over me as I sleep.
In the name of Jesus, amen.

JESUS WAS THINKING OF ME...

We do this by keeping our eyes on Jesus, the Champion who initiates and perfects our faith. Because of the joy awaiting Him, He endured the cross, disregarding its shame. Now He is seated in the place of honor beside God's throne.

Hebrews 12:2 NLT

You are called to keep your eyes on Jesus, the Author and the Perfector of your faith. Jesus is the one who gives you faith to believe. He initiates the faith; without Him, you would not even have the ability to believe. He is also the one who perfects your faith along the journey. Fix your gaze on Him. Behold the cross.

Everything in the Christian faith should point you to Jesus. He is what everything else hinges on. He is the One who holds everything. He is the anchor for your soul. **Jesus endured the cross because of the joy awaiting Him. That joy was you.** He endured the taunts, the beatings, and the nails in His hands and feet because He knew that waiting on the other side of the pain of the cross was a relationship with you.

Jesus gazed across the generations and saw *you*. He saw everything you would need to live your life, and He purchased it all at the cross. Whatever you face in your life, you can look past the storm, to the other side. In the middle, keep your gaze on Jesus. During every storm, there is a time when the clouds will clear and the light will shine again. Let Jesus's grace, His mercy, and His love be your firm foundation. You can endure because of the joy on the other side. Jesus is at the throne and He awaits in anticipation to pour His love out on you!

Today, I pray...

Father, Jesus will never leave me nor forsake me. Cause me to keep my gaze fixed upon Him. Put my mind on Jesus—I submit to You my entire will. I look forward to this day inside Your perfect purpose! Amen.

So Glad God's in Charge

"For My thoughts are not your thoughts, nor are your ways My ways," says the Lord. "For as the heavens are higher than the earth, so are My ways higher than your ways, and My thoughts than your thoughts.

Isaiah 55:8-9 NKJV

"My thoughts are not your thoughts."

Aren't we thankful that God is more intelligent than we are? Aren't we thankful that His ways are not our ways, that His will is perfect and holy and just?

This knowledge comes in handy when we don't understand what God is doing. Let's say He allowed something sad to happen to us or to someone we love, or maybe He allowed something to occur with our job or livelihood. What we need to understand is that whatever He's allowing, He is doing it for His own good purposes. **Because you belong to God through Jesus, anything that happens to you, He controls.** You are His child—you can trust that He knows what's happening and He is working the situation for your ultimate good.

Yes, the enemy can attack, oppress and annoy you, but even that is allowed by and controlled by God. Look at the story of Job—God gave satan permission to all but *kill* him! Job never lost his faith. Let Job be our role model in times of suffering. When you enter a tough time, ask God to reveal what needs to be done to correct it. If you need chastisement, or if your suffering helps someone else—ask God to reveal it to you. **Never stop praying and worshipping God in the storm.** And always accept on faith that He knows what He's doing.

Tonight, I pray...

Dear Father, I thank You that Your ways are not my ways and that Your thoughts are high above me. I thank You that human beings don't run the universe. Father, continue to teach me this truth, that every day, I understand more and more what You were doing. You said we should ask You for wisdom, so I ask for the wisdom of God, in Jesus' holy name. Amen.

I LOVE THE GOOD SHEPHERD

"Fear not, little flock, for it is your Father's good pleasure to give you the kingdom."

Luke 12:32 ESV

God does not want us to live our lives in constant fear. His word says that His perfect love drives out all fear. There is no room in His love for fear. Fear is a thief. It will paralyze your life and cause you to make decisions that are not God's will for you.

When Jesus died on the cross, He destroyed the power of fear. Colossians 2:15 says that Jesus disarmed the rulers and authorities of darkness, making a spectacle out of them at the cross. **Fear has absolutely no power in your life unless you give in to it.**

Fear never comes from God. God gives you power, love, and a sound mind, so if you are struggling with thoughts of fear, you can know it is never from God. Since fear is not from God, you know it is from the devil. Jesus told us that the devil is a liar and there is no truth in him, so you can know there is no truth in the lies that fear is whispering in your ears. Remember, God's perfect love drives out fear.

You can live free from fear because you know that if Jesus would die for you, there is not one thing He wouldn't do for you. You can trust in His perfect love for you. You can know that the Father longs to lavish you with His love. He waits in anticipation to give you good things. If earthly parents know how to give good gifts to their children, and enjoy doing it, how much more does your Father in heaven enjoy and know how to provide you with good gifts! **Fear not, little flock, Jesus is your Good Shepherd.**

Today, I pray...

Heavenly Father, thank You that I am in Your flock. You called me and I heard Your voice. Hallelujah! Make my paths straight and cause me to perform Your perfect will. I want to be like You! Amen.

GOD IS ECHAD

*"I do not pray for these alone, but also for those who will believe in Me through their word; **that they all may be one,** as You, Father, are in Me, and I in You; that they also may be one in Us, that the world may believe that You sent Me.*

John chapter 17: 20-21

*"Hear, O Israel: The LORD our God, the **LORD is one!"***

Deuteronomy 6:4-5

Reading the Bible in English is a wonderful blessing. As we grow in our faith, we begin to look deeper, seeking out the Hebrew and Greek meanings of the original texts, in the original speakers' languages, with cultural context to further understand what God is saying to us in His Word.

Deuteronomy 6:4 - note the original Hebrew

echad YHVH Elohim YHVH Yisrael Shema

Literal translation

Hear Israel YHVH is our God YHVH is One.

Today's verses bring me great joy because I have learned about ECHAD. Pronounced, "e-KAHD", this is Hebrew for what our English translation calls, "one." The word *echad* means "a compound unity."[14] This boggled the minds of the learned Jews when Jesus came into His ministry. Even today, Orthodox Jews are offended that God used it in Deuteronomy 6:4 (among other places) to express the plural-nature of Father, Son, Holy Spirit. **God was expressing Himself as Tri-une from the beginning!**

95

In Deuteronomy, God says, "YHVH* is our God (*Elohim*), YHVH* is One (*echad*)." This is important because when Jesus spoke this verse in the New Testament, **He quoted the Old Testament verse in Hebrew and called Himself ONE –** "echad" – with the Father. Then, He says it is His prayer that all of us who believe in Him will also become ONE (echad) with Him as He is ONE (echad) with the Father. (!!!!) **Imagine being ONE with the Creator in the same way Jesus is!**

*YHVH is God's name in the original language of the Bible. Pronounced, *yod-hay-vav-hay*, each word is the actual name of that Hebrew letter seen in the pictogram.

Yod'-hay ה -vav ו -hay ה , reads right to left   יהוה

God's name has been hidden for now[15] because there are no vowels given. Hebrew scholars say His name as **Yod-Hay-Vav-Hay.** English Bible scholars have given us "Jehovah" and "YahWeh," among others, as they attempt to guess what the vowels might be. As with everything having to do with Jesus, He knows when you are calling Him, no matter if we don't know how to pronounce it!

Tonight, I pray...

Father, just keep teaching me more about You. I want to know more! In Jesus' holy name!

25

JESUS MAKES ME MERRY

These things I have spoken to you, that in Me you may have peace. In the world you will have tribulation; but be of good cheer, I have overcome the world."

John 16:33 NKJV

Even when the world around you is shaken, if everything is broken and falls apart, **you can still have peace.** God never promised us life would be easy. He never promised we would get everything we ever wanted. Jesus said there will be tribulation, but you do not have to face these trials as the world faces them. You do not have to be shaken and afraid.

Isaiah 8:12-14 says, *"don't call everything a conspiracy, like they do, and don't live in dread of what frightens them. Make the LORD of Heaven's Armies holy in your life. He is the one you should fear. He is the one who should make you tremble. He will keep you safe."*

Build your faith on Jesus even more when the world is in chaos seeking protection and comfort. They turn to other religions, consult psychics, you name it. You, beloved, will be a light that shines into that darkness. The world will look at you and wonder why you are so calm amid the turmoil. **You will be able to tell them it is because of Jesus.**

Be of good cheer. Even though there will be tribulation, you can be full of joy! You can still dance in the rain and chase snowflakes, enjoy life and be filled with laughter. Be merry in your heart at all times. Not because the times are always good, but **because Jesus is always good,** and He has overcome this world.

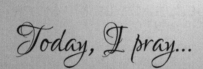

Today, I pray...

Jesus, You are my firm foundation. I build my house on You, and I will not be shaken. You make my life merry no matter what a mess the world is in or the chaos around me. You are beautiful and holy and perfect! Amen.

Keep Calm and Trust God

... [Jesus] poured water into a basin and began to wash the disciples' feet, and to wipe them with the towel with which He was girded. Then He came to Simon Peter. And Peter said to Him, "Lord, are You washing my feet?" Jesus answered and said to him, "What I am doing you do not understand now, but you will know after this."

John 13: 5-7 NKJV

"You do not understand what I am doing now, but later you will understand."

When I was a new Christian and going through a tough trial, I slumped into my chair and prayed to God, "please let me open the Bible at random, select a verse, and have it be meaningful to this mess I'm in." Then I selected with my eyes closed John 13:7, "You do not understand what I am doing now, but later you will understand"! **Imagine reading that line after what I just prayed!**

I never forgot that moment and I never forgot that teaching. That being, no matter what is going on in my life, I know I belong to God, so He is in control of it all. **All I have to do is trust and carry on.**

God is always doing things that confound mankind. What an amazing thing that He would create this entire race with Adam and Eve. What an amazing thing that He would be born of a virgin so He can put His full goodness into a human. Confounding man is a great way to display God's omnipotence, wouldn't you say?!

So, when anything comes your way, good or bad, remember that it is for a purpose. You can ask God to reveal to you if you've sinned or gone astray, but always trust He isn't surprised to find you in a predicament! Ask Him to help you out of it and pray for His will to be done with it. It really takes the burden off of you once you realize that God is in control and not you.

Tonight, I pray...

Father, remind me of this every day, that You're working Your will in my life. Remind me to ask You to do so, because that brings glory and honor and majesty to Your name. I turn over my life to You. Make my dreams and ambitions line up with Yours every day.
In Jesus' name, amen.

26

It is Finished

When He had received the drink, Jesus said, "It is finished."
With that, He bowed His head and gave up His spirit.
John 19:30 NIV

It is finished! Three of my favorite words in the Bible. Jesus completed everything that needed to be completed for me to have a relationship with Him. He had fulfilled the prophecies of the Old Testament about the Messiah. Now there is nothing left for you to do except rest in His finished work for you.

As Christians, we spend a lot of time striving and frustrated, trying to *earn* something from God that we already have, that is, His love and His blessings. **When you try to add to what Jesus has already done, it is like saying that His death was not enough.** He was the perfect sacrifice. Isaiah 53:5 says, *"But he was pierced for our transgressions, he was crushed for our iniquities; the punishment that brought us peace was on him, and by his wounds we are healed."*

You can do nothing to earn God's affections for you or His blessings on your life. **Jesus paid it all. His blood was enough.** His Word says that every promise we receive is through Jesus. Not through your being good enough, going to church enough, or reading your Bible enough, but through Jesus's finished work at the cross.

All you need to do is believe that Jesus has already paid the price. If someone wants to give you a gift, but you insist on working for or paying for it, it is no longer a gift. You cannot ever do enough to pay for what Jesus has done for you, and God does not want you to. He wants you to freely and graciously receive His love, and His blessings poured out on your life. Any time you have something you are facing, just ask yourself, did Jesus take care of this at the cross? The answer to that question is always yes. Lean into Him and know that **He loves you because He wants to,** not because of something you can or have done.

Today, I pray...

Father, the war is over, and the enemy has been defeated. You have won. Death is defeated. I will keep my eyes on You always. I will rest in You! Please show me how to rest — grow my faith! Amen.

Our Upside-Down World

At that time Jesus answered and said, "I thank You, Father, Lord of heaven and earth, that You have hidden these things from the wise and prudent and have revealed them to babes."

Matthew 11: 25-26

There are some crazy things being said on the news and social media these days. Things that are opposite of what God taught us. Why can't people understand that You can't make something true just by redefining the word. A blue crayon doesn't become pink simply because you *feel like it should be pink.* There are hard facts in this world and when we hear the opposite being shared by multiple voices, it can be quite frustrating. This is where this Bible verse comes in.

When we became followers of Jesus Christ through our faith in His sacrifice, the Holy Spirit indwelled us and He constantly gives us discernment. **God reveals truth to us because we belong to Him.** These very same truths are hidden from unbelievers. This is as God wants it for His purposes. They simply are incapable of knowing the Truth!

So, what can we do about it?

Tonight, I pray...

Father, I thank You that you have hidden the wisdom of
God from those who are lost. Thank You for revealing Your
truth to me and my brothers and sisters in Jesus. Help me
to remember this when I become frustrated with the
upside-down world we live in. And remind me to pray for
the Lord of the harvest because the fields are ripe.
Remind me to pray for Your will to be done on earth as it is
in heaven. In the name of Jesus Christ, amen.

27

MAKE JESUS YOUR ONE THING

Taste and see that the LORD is good.
Oh, the joys of those who take refuge in Him!

Psalm 34:8 NLT

Taste and see that the Lord is good! Jesus is the best thing that will ever happen to your life! He satisfies more than any of the richest of foods that you will ever taste. Once you have come to know His character and spend time with Him and get to know His love for you, you will never hunger for anything else. Jesus becomes the One thing you need.

David said he thirsted for Him in a dry and weary land where there was no water. Isaiah 55:1-2 the Bible says, *"Is anyone thirsty? Come and drink—even if you have no money! Come, take your choice of wine or milk—it's all free! Why spend your money on food that does not give you strength? Why pay for food that does you no good? Listen to Me, and you will eat what is good. You will enjoy the finest food."*

When you make Jesus your one thing, He brings joy to your life. When you make Him your refuge, your strong tower, your place of safety, He will show you things that you could only imagine in your wildest imaginations. Your life will never be the same.

105

You can trust Him with your life. Psalm 91:1-2 says, *"Those who live in the shelter of the Most High will find rest in the shadow of the Almighty. This I declare about the LORD: He alone is my refuge, my place of safety; He is my God, and I trust Him."*

When you make your home in Jesus, you find rest in Him. Jesus is the answer to everything that you struggle with and He knows what it is like to be human. We see Jesus in the Bible weeping over friends, showing compassion to the sick, bringing freedom to the captives. We see Him eating meals with sinners and bringing rest to the weary and burdened. These are not just stories in a book about Jesus; this is real life. **The invitation to know Jesus is for all who will come,** taste, and see, just one time in His presence, and you will see that He is not just good, but He is magnificent.

Today, I pray...

Heavenly Father, I have tasted and see that the Lord is good! I want more of You! Today and every day, fill me with Your Holy Spirit and teach me how to spread the Good News of Jesus to those in my path. Amen.

IT WILL BE WELL WITH ME

"But this is what I commanded them, saying, 'Obey My voice, and I will be your God, and you shall be My people. And walk in all the ways that I have commanded you, that it may be well with you.'"
Jeremiah 7:23 NKJV

In the book of Jeremiah, God wanted the prophet to express to the people of Israel that in order for them to know Him, they would need to walk in His ways.

Why?

God wasn't arbitrarily assigning laws. Think about it, God was and is holy, perfect, and there is no blight or mark on Him. Mankind is flesh, which means we are flawed and sinful. **Unclean cannot share space with the clean.** This is a parameter set up by God from the beginning of the world. Because of this, God gave commandments to teach the people of Israel how to become holy in the sight of God.

We are Christians saved by faith in Jesus. Performing the laws of God do not save us from hell. Because of this, this Old Testament verse serves to remind us that we obey God *because we want to be His people.* We *want* to obey our Father in heaven. *Because* He is our father. This is the way God created the father-son / parent-child relationship. No matter how perverted it has become in the 21st Century, the fact remains that in God's design, the parent loves the child sacrificially and the child loves the parent with holy fear. This is good and proper, hallelujah!

Tonight, I pray...

Father, I want to be among Your people. Teach me how to walk in Your ways so things will be well with me. I know I'm saved by faith in Jesus, but I also know that performing Your will blesses Your heart. Father, I want to please You. Teach me how and enable me to hear what You are saying. Amen.

I Know Him!

So you also are complete through your union with Christ,
who is the head over every ruler and authority.

Colossians 2:10 NLT

You are complete through your union with Christ. We spend a lot of time searching for things to complete us, whether it be fame, material things, people, the way we look, education, etc. We pay lots of money and sometimes go through a lot of pain to find these things. Sometimes we even compromise our beliefs and morals because we want to feel complete.

We want to feel needed and important. We need to know that we matter. The world gives us the idea that this can be found in temporal things. The constant barrage of information on social media, television, and billboards beckons us to find something better than we already have. Something newer, shinier, younger. It is a constant cycle of chasing *things* that make promises to us, and those promises keep eluding us. **There is only one person that can complete you, and that is Jesus.**

When you have Jesus, He satisfies that search to be fulfilled. Jesus approves of you, He accepts you. You are valuable to

Him. **Jesus is all you need.** Even if everything and everyone else were taken away, you would still be complete in Him. He is the One you have been searching for all your life. Jesus is the head and the authority over everything in heaven and earth. He is above everything. He holds everything together. He created the whole universe. He is the Word of God become flesh.

The Bible says to seek His kingdom first, and all other things will be added to you. **When He is what you want the most, He will put His desires in your heart.** You will start to think like He thinks, and dream as He dreams, and love like He loves. You will never regret making Jesus the lover of your soul. When He appears again to take us home, you will be able to say, "I know Him"!

Today, I pray...

Heavenly Father, thank You that I am complete because I know Jesus. I want to continue to grow into Your image. Teach me how to be a better disciple of Jesus, to imitate Him. I love You and I need You. Amen.

Obedience Shows Love

"If you love Me, keep my commandments."
John 14:15 NKJV

It is a beautiful thing to know that Jesus said, *if you love me keep my commandments.* **Jesus proved to us multiple times that He and the Father are One.** This means God's commandments are Jesus' commandments. Jesus saved us from eternal death, but to show our love for Him, we keep His commandments.

New Christians often wonder, what are Jesus' commandments? In the New Testament, Jesus summed them up by saying, "Do unto others as you would have them do unto you." He said this sums up the Old Testament, and He says it should be obeyed. **Jesus did not come into the world to destroy the Old Testament, but rather, to fulfill it.** The New Covenant and the Old Covenant are perfect.

In Old Testament days, God's children were instructed to obey the Law because it enabled them to pass muster on judgement day. **Christians' faith in Jesus is their ticket to eternity with God.** Christians obey God's commandments because it shows Jesus that we love Him!

Tonight, I pray...

Jesus, I love You and I need You. Forgive me for being rebellious and forgive me for being lazy. I don't read the Bible as much as I should. I don't pray as often as I should. And I surely don't ask You what You want me to do or study up on the commandments of God as much as I ought to. Father, please show me what to do. Teach me Your ways. I love You and I want to keep Your commandments in a way that pleases You. In Jesus' holy name. Amen.

$$29$$

No Weapon Formed Against Me

The thief comes only in order to steal and kill and destroy. I came that they may have and enjoy life, and have it in abundance (to the full, till it overflows).

John 10:10 AMPC

The enemy of your soul has one purpose, which is to steal, kill, and destroy. He uses many different tactics to do this in our lives. Sometimes, he uses sickness in our physical bodies. He sometimes uses your mind to attack you with fear, anxiety, depression, doubt, shame, and insecurity. He attacks your relationships with your spouse, friends, children, and primarily your relationship with God.

He wants you to believe that God is not good, that He is not out to help you, that He does not care about you, or maybe he causes you to question if God is real at all. **He wants you to question God's faithfulness.** He wants to paralyze you and make you unable to be any good to God's Kingdom.

The Word of God tells us that no weapon formed against you will prosper. The enemy may form the weapon, but it will not prosper. Jesus always steps in at the right moment to kick the devil in the teeth. You never have to spend your time yelling at the devil; just call upon Jesus. **Jesus makes demons bow and brings peace to your life.**

You are an overcomer in Jesus. **The same Spirit that raised Jesus from the dead lives in you.** You do not have to put up with the devil whispering lies into your mind all the time; you have the authority to tell Him to shut up. Turn your face to Jesus and remember the devil can roar, but when you are a child of God, He cannot harm you. Jesus is always in control of life, even when it may look like the enemy is winning. In everything in the life of a believer, Jesus has the final word. Do not let the enemy scare you. Do not give Him a second thought. Jesus reigns and will reign for all days now and forever!

Today, I pray...

Father in heaven, hallowed be Your name. Thank You for protecting me from satan. Forgive me for sometimes falling into despair and listening to his whispering. Remind me in these times that my hope is in You and that I trust and love YOU alone. In Jesus' name, amen.

Help Them Speak to God

"Call to Me, and I will answer you, and show you great and mighty things, which you do not know."

Jeremiah 33:3 NKJV

***Call to me...* this is an amazing thing**. I know plenty of people who have no interest in knowing God better, but whenever I meet someone who *does* want to know Him better, they are not sure how to start a conversation with Him. I want to share with you what God taught me about this very thing.

A young woman came up to me some years back and felt she was too dirty, too filthy, too gross to even say hello to God. After ministering to her that she wasn't, I sat with her, held her hands, and said, **"I'll pray with you.** Just repeat after me." She was literally terrified, shaking her head and arguing with me, but finally, she bowed down and closed her eyes.

I told her, "Just say, 'hi, God.'" She did so, and the floodgates opened. **She began to cry with force,** and all the pain and agony she held inside came out. See, she had been raped and never told a soul. When her tears ceased, she explained to me that the assault caused her to feel ruined forever.

See how the devil made her think she was unsaveable?
If you are willing, add this to your life mission, to help someone speak to God who thinks they are too unclean to do so. The devil is deceiving many people out there—maybe God will send you some that only need to say, "Hi, God…"

Tonight, I pray…

Father, I want to help people speak to You. First, teach me how to better communicate with You, how to speak to You as naturally as I would speak to someone in the flesh. And then send me someone that You want me to talk to about You and nudge me hard enough that I'll know You're sending them. Teach me how to discern Your voice, because I want to do Your will above all else's. Thank You, in Jesus' name.

God is Magnificent!

My response is to get down on my knees before the Father, this magnificent Father who parcels out all heaven and earth. I ask Him to strengthen you by His Spirit—not a brute strength but a glorious inner strength—that Christ will live in you as you open the door and invite Him in. And I ask Him that with both feet planted firmly on love, you'll be able to take in with all followers of Jesus the extravagant dimensions of Christ's love. Reach out and experience the breadth! Test its length! Plumb the depths! Rise to the heights! Live full lives, full in the fullness of God.

Ephesians 3:14-19 TM

God is the magnificent Father of all heaven and all earth. He is the creator of everything and has unlimited resources to take care of you. We fall on our knees in awe of Him. God gives you His glorious inner strength by His Spirit that lives every moment inside of you. As you invite Jesus into your heart and you put your trust in Him, you will begin to experience His life in you. You will start to experience His love for yourself. You can plant both of your feet firmly on that love.

God's love is a steady and firm foundation. As you invite Him in and focus on His love for you, you will see how extravagant His love is for you. He invites you to experience the breadth of it, see how long it is, dive into the depths of it, and rise to the heights of it—this unbelievable, incomprehensible love of Christ.

Jesus's love will cause you to see things differently. You will treat people differently. Jesus will give you compassion for people that you did not have before. When you experience His love, you cannot just keep it to yourself; you will want to share it with others. It becomes a continual flow. His love flows from Him to you, and then from you to back to Him, and that love connection overflows to everyone around you and causes them to have the experience with His love.

When you open your life and let the love and light of Jesus take over, you will be utterly amazed at what God will do, first in you and then through you. He will take you places you never dreamed you would go and cause you to be able to do things that you never dreamed you would do. A life lived with Jesus is a life of adventure, a life full of joy and peace. The most famous and affluent of people are still searching for something they feel is missing in their lives, and you have that something living and breathing inside of you. They are waiting for you to share Him. Let's do it!

Today, I pray...

Father, I want everyone to know You! I have been forever changed by You! Please show me how to share this amazing truth with the world and give me courage to even try. Thank You, my God and King! Amen.

Jesus Made the World

In the beginning God created the heavens and the earth. The earth was without form, and void; and darkness was on the face of the deep. And the Spirit of God was hovering over the face of the waters. Then God said, "Let there be light"; and there was light. And God saw the light, that it was good; and God divided the light from the darkness. God called the light Day, and the darkness He called Night. So the evening and the morning were the first day.

Genesis 1:1-5 NKJV

God spoke the world into existence.

This alone is amazing and incomprehensible, but let's add another element that blows my mind.

Jesus is the word of God. John 1:14 NKJV, *And the Word became flesh and dwelt among us, and we beheld His glory, the glory as of the only begotten of the Father, full of grace and truth.*

So, Jesus created the world!

Do you see? The Father, the Son, and the Holy Spirit are ONE, *echad* (see Day 24), and it pleased God for Jesus to bring the world into being. Doesn't this make sense since we learned already in the scriptures that the world was made for Him, through Him, and by Him?

Colossians 1:17 NKJV: *All things were created through Him and for Him. And He is before all things, and in Him all things consist.*

Tonight, I pray...

Father, You are amazing! I ask You to remind me every day and every night how utterly amazing and wonderful You are. I believe You created this world and I want to spend eternity with You. Amen and Amen.

31

GOOD MORNING!

If then you were raised with Christ, seek those things which are above, where Christ is, sitting at the right hand of God. Set your mind on things above, not on things on the earth. For you died, and your life is hidden with Christ in God. When Christ, who is our life, appears, then you will also appear with Him in glory.
Colossians 3:1-4 NKJV

Keep your thoughts on things above, not things below. Keep your mind focused on Jesus, not on your problems, cares, anxieties, and worries. **This is a lot easier said than done.** You must practice. Every time your mind starts to wander to a place of fear or worry, you must try your very best to turn your thoughts to God.

Galatians 2:20 says, "I live, yet not I but Christ who lives in me." **So not only are you in Christ, but Christ is in you.** It is a complete union. The Bible says you live and move and have your being in Christ. This doesn't mean you constantly have to be praying or reading your Bible, but that in everything you do throughout your day, Christ is there with you. Invite Him to interact with you. Practice His presence by talking to Him about everything you are doing. If you are at work, the grocery store, or walking down the street, allow

Jesus to be involved in your conversations and decisions. If something is plaguing your mind, don't wait until you can sit down for a long prayer; whisper a prayer to Him right where you are.

There will be one day when everything changes. When the skies open and the Son of God, our Savior, and King will come down, **and in the twinkling of an eye,** we will be taken to heaven with Him and live in His presence, seeing Him face to face for eternity. He will be revealed to all, and you will be revealed as His child. We do our best to be aware of Christ in us, our hope of glory until that day. We fix our thoughts on Him and carry His peace and love and hope with us everywhere we go, and we share Him with everyone we meet. Let's live like we mean it!

Today, I pray...

Heavenly Father, I want to seek You. Today and every day, cause me to seek Your face and Your presence. I don't want the world, I want You! Amen.

Good Evening!

He who dwells in the secret place of the Most High shall abide under the shadow of the Almighty.

Psalm 91:1 NKJV

The secret place of the Most High.

When you study this phrase in Hebrew, it is a sense of a bird tucking her young under her wing and holding them against her breast.

God longs to hold us close, right up against His breast. When we seek this secret place, this place of communication, where we study His word and we seek His will, and we pray daily for His guidance, we find we are resting in the shadow of the Almighty and we know that He is our refuge. This communication gives us confidence in Him.

If you call your friend daily, you know that friend better. If you spend every minute with him/her, then you really get to know them better. God wants constant communication with us! **We can grow in our faith simply by remaining in prayer and studying His word!**

Tonight, I pray...

Father, I want to read this to You right now in Jesus' name.

He who dwells in the secret place of the Most High shall
abide under the shadow of the Almighty.
I will say of the Lord, "He is my refuge and my fortress;
My God, in Him I will trust."
Surely He shall deliver you from the snare of the fowler
And from the perilous pestilence.

He shall cover you with His feathers,
And under His wings you shall take refuge;
His truth shall be your shield and buckler.

You shall not be afraid of the terror by night,
Nor of the arrow that flies by day,
Nor of the pestilence that walks in darkness,
Nor of the destruction that lays waste at noonday.

A thousand may fall at your side,
And ten thousand at your right hand;
But it shall not come near you.
Only with your eyes shall you look,
And see the reward of the wicked.

Father, I just read Psalm 91:1-8 to You and I ask You to
make this true in my life. May every word of this be true, in
Jesus' holy name. Amen!

"I have said these things to you so that, united with Me, you may have PEACE. In the world, you have trouble. But be brave! I have conquered the world!"

John 16:33

About the Authors

Gina Lynn Murray

Bestselling author and aspiring speaker Gina Lynn Murray lives with her husband and fur babies in Missouri. Gina's first book, *One Trembling Heart, Out of Darkness Into Light,* was birthed from a journey laced with severe anxiety, fear and depression. *One Trembling Heart* hit Amazon's bestseller list, receiving rave reviews right off the bat. It is Gina's heart to pour God's love into broken vessels and see His children healed. Gina has a weekly podcast/ YouTube series called "Wednesday's At the Well". You can read more about Gina and see her videos or listen to her podcast on her website, onetremblingheart.com.

LittleRoniPublishers.com

Ellen Sallas

Ellen is Editorial Director and founder of Little Roni Publishers, LLC (an independent traditional publishing company), as well as founder of The Author's Mentor (a free-advice, low-cost book services company that has helped over 400 authors publish more than 500 books). Ellen is a widely sought keynote speaker for book clubs, schools, and education organizations all over the south, including Beeson Divinity School at Samford University and the SCWC. Under the pen name Ellen C. Maze, she authored the 2020 Gold Medal Winner Reader's Favorite International Book Award & #1 bestselling Christian Thriller *Rabbit: Chasing Beth Rider*, among many other titles in different genres. See more at www.ellencmaze.com & www.LittleRoniPublishers.com.

Check out Gina's NEW RELEASE!

One Trembling Heart, Out of Darkness Into the Light: A Journey from Paralyzing Anxiety to Finding Rest

In softcover and eBook!

Publisher Statement

LRP FAITH

Imprint of Little Roni Publishers

Clanton, Alabama

www.littleronipublishers.com

Little Roni Publishers' *Faith* Imprint has been created and set apart to the glory of Jesus Christ, our God and King.

This company is unashamedly sold-out and head over heels for Jesus. If you would like help to know Him or need prayer, email us at submissionsLRP@gmail.com.

Isaiah 58:12 | Galatians 2:20

Endnotes

[1] *Little "s" satan.* Little Roni Publishers will not capitalize the devil's name. The deceiver is defeated; may as well reflect that in its proper nouns. ~ The Editor

[2] Genesis 1:3 – And God *said 'Let there be Light.'...*
[3] John 1:1.
[4] John 10:27.
[5] 1 John 1: 8-10, If we claim to be without sin, we deceive ourselves and the truth is not in us. If we confess our sins, he is faithful and just and will forgive us our sins and purify us from all unrighteousness. If we claim we have not sinned, we make him out to be a liar and his word is not in us.

[6] Genesis 6:3, Then the Lord said, "My Spirit will not contend with humans forever, for they are mortal; their days will be a hundred and twenty years."

[7] This is an involved study, but in short, during "the Rapture," Jesus does not touch down to earth, but comes in the clouds to gather all believers to Him from all ends of the earth. After that is the "Second Coming," the timing of which is what Jesus refers to when He says, "No one knows the day or the hour." We can know the Rapture is close because of the signs He warned us of, but of the Second Coming, no one knows, now even the Son. There will be no another chance for unbelievers to repent once He return to earth. The Bible explains that people on earth who remain after the Rapture, have chance to be saved during Great Tribulation, under Antichrist's reign. Once the Lord comes, it is too late for them to repent. Revelation teaches that they won't want to, anyway.

[8] "For we must all appear before the judgment seat of Christ, so that each of us may receive what is due us for the things done while in the body, whether good or bad." – 2 Corinthians 5:10. The word for judgment here is from the root word "bema" in the Greek. This is a seat where rewards and punishments can be handed out. In this judgment of believers, we will be rewarded or not rewarded for what we did after we received Christ as savior. It is important to distinguish that this is not a judgment of your salvation but of your works done after you received salvation, derived from, crosswalk.com/faith/bible-study/what-is-the-great-white-throne-judgment.html

[9] 2 Corinthians 10:5, "We demolish arguments and every pretension that sets itself up against the knowledge of God, and we take captive every thought to make it obedient to Christ."

[10] 5G and 6G technology generate billions in revenue. When researching anything that makes money for the elites, you must use God-given discernment to see through the lies. Real science says these microwaves are dangerous. Common sense should reveal this to everyone, but it doesn't. The lie is huge. One explanatory link among hundreds is here: https://www.sciencetimes.com/articles/20602/20190422/wifi-may-cause-irreversible-damage-to-the-brain.htm

[11] Expect 6G by the year 2030, when everything will be available instantly with zero wait times. After that, we won't need to invent new terms to describe it. https://www.lifewire.com/6g-wireless-4685524 When Will 6G Come Out? It's been typical for a new mobile network standard to take the spotlight every decade or so. That means that 6G networks might roll out sometime around 2030.

[12] Matthew 18:10, NKJV, "Take heed that you do not despise one of these little ones, for I say to you that in heaven their angels always see the face of My Father who is in heaven.

[13] James 1:5, NKJV: If any of you lacks wisdom, let him ask of God, who gives to all liberally and without reproach, and it will be given to him.

[14] Echad – a great teaching is found at, https://hebrew4christians.com/Scripture/Shloshah-Asar_Ikkarim/Yachid/yachid.html

[15] God will reveal His name at the End. Revelation 3:12 "He who overcomes, I will make him a pillar in the temple of My God, and he shall go out no more. I will write on him the name of My God and the name of the city of My God, the New Jerusalem, which comes down out of heaven from My God. And *I will write on him* My new name."